Grammar Galaxy

Adventures in Language Arts

Blue Star

Melanie Wilson, Ph.D.
Rebecca Mueller, Illustrator

GRAMMAR GALAXY: BLUE STAR
Copyright © 2020 by Fun to Learn Books

All rights reserved. No part of this book may be reproduced or transmitted in any form or by any means without written permission from the author: grammargalaxybooks@gmail.com.

ISBN: 978-1-7354939-0-9

Table of Contents

Table of Contents 3

A Note to Teachers 5

A Note to Students 6

Unit I: Adventures in Literature 7

Chapter 1: Literature Unit Study 8

Chapter 2: Tone & Mood 13

Chapter 3: Short Stories 18

Chapter 4: Allusions 22

Chapter 5: Narrative Poems 26

Chapter 6: Nonfiction Reading 33

Chapter 7: Urban Legends 37

Chapter 8: Shakespeare 41

Chapter 9: Satire 45

Unit II: Adventures in Spelling & Vocabulary 50

Chapter 10: Science Vocabulary 51

Chapter 11: Oxymorons 56

Chapter 12: Onomatopoeia 61

Chapter 13: British Spelling 66

Chapter 14: British Vocabulary 71

Chapter 15: Confused Vocabulary 77

Chapter 16: Vocabulary Mnemonics 84

Chapter 17: Prefixes, Suffixes & Root Words 88

Chapter 18: Spelling High-Frequency Words 93

Unit IV: Adventures in Grammar 97

Chapter 19: Diagramming 98

Chapter 20: Grammatical Mood 104

Chapter 21: Infinitives 109

Chapter 22: Progressive Verb Tense 114

Chapter 23: Adverbial Clauses & Phrases 118

Chapter 24: Relative Pronouns 123

Chapter 25: Misplaced Modifiers 128

Chapter 26: Dashes & Parentheses 133

Unit V: Adventures in Composition & Speaking 137

Chapter 27: Parallel Structure 138

Chapter 28: Morning Pages 143

Chapter 29: Passive Voice 148

Chapter 30: Profile Essays 153

Chapter 31: Writing Summaries 159

Chapter 32: Persuasive Speaking 164

Chapter 33: News Articles 169

Chapter 34: Compare-and-Contrast Essays 174

Chapter 35: Slogans 178

Chapter 36: Gift Poems 183

About the Author 187

About the Illustrator 188

Appendix: Answers to Comprehension Questions 189

A Note to Teachers

I'm passionate about language arts. I love to read, write, and speak. As a homeschooling mom, I wanted my own children and my friends' children to share my passion. Over the years, I found aspects of many different curricula that clicked with my students. But I never found something that did everything I wanted a complete curriculum for elementary students to do:

- Use the most powerful medium to teach language arts: story
- Give the why of language arts to motivate students
- Teach to mastery rather than drill the same concepts year after year

I felt called to create my own fast, easy, and fun curriculum for teachers who want to see students succeed in language arts.

Grammar Galaxy: Blue Star is for students who have mastered the concepts taught in *Grammar Galaxy: Red Star*. It is intended for both independent reading and as a read aloud for a family.

When reading aloud, share the synonyms for vocabulary words given in the text. Following each story, there are questions to ask students to check for comprehension. The answers are given in the Appendix.

With your help, students should complete the corresponding mission in the *Mission Manual* before moving on to the next story. Classroom teachers may wish to create customized missions.

My hope is that your students will accept the call to be guardians of Grammar Galaxy.

Melanie Wilson

A Note to Students

I need your help. Grammar Galaxy is in trouble. The Gremlin is working hard to keep kids from reading, learning new words, and spelling correctly. He also wants to keep them from writing and public speaking. He knows that if he succeeds, the English language will be weak, and life will be miserable.

Here is how you can help defeat the Gremlin. First, read each chapter in the text, paying attention to the vocabulary words that are in **bold text**. Note the synonym (word with similar meaning) that is given for each. Then make sure you can answer the discussion questions at the end of each chapter. If you can't, review the text, and if you still need help, check the Appendix at the back of the book. Finally, complete the mission in your mission manual with the same number as the chapter in this book.

I'm proud to have you join us as a guardian of the galaxy!

Melanie Wilson

Unit I: Adventures in Literature

Chapter 1

The king's face was red when he joined the queen in the sunroom one morning.

"What's wrong?" she asked.

"I just got off the phone with the king of History Galaxy." The queen urged him to continue his explanation. "He was furious because of a letter I sent."

"You sent him a letter? That was so thoughtful. People don't send nearly as many letters anymore," the queen mused.

"I did not send him a letter!" the king said loudly.

Chapter 1: Literature Unit Study

The queen flinched and continued tentatively. "But you just said you sent him a letter."

"No," the king answered harshly. "I said the History king was upset because of a letter I sent—"

"Exactly! That's what I said," the queen said, frowning.

"I didn't send it," the king said, trying to calm himself.

The queen noticed his effort at self-control and responded in kind. "Okay. What did the letter say?"

"It said Grammar Galaxy is the most important galaxy in the universe. It said that History Galaxy must submit to my rule or face the consequences."

The queen's mouth fell open. When she collected herself, she said, "I think that was rather rude of you."

"I did not write that!" the king said, his voice rising again.

"You didn't write that the History king should submit to you?" The king nodded, grateful that the queen was understanding. "Why did you tell me that you wrote that then?" she asked indignantly.

The king was about to lose his temper when the butler appeared. "Sire, the king of Science Galaxy is waiting to speak with you via video conference in your study. And if I may say so, he did not seem happy."

"That's just great!" the king said, raising his hands in exasperation.

As he left the room, the queen called after him, "You should have thought twice before sending those letters." The king shook his head in frustration but continued walking.

At dinner that evening, the king was in a foul mood. When Ellen commented on it, the queen explained. Your father sent a rude letter to some other galaxy kings and now he is paying the price for it," she said **sanctimoniously**.

The king's eyes narrowed as he considered how to respond. "I did not send any rude letters," he stated calmly.

✯ ✯ ✯ ✯ ✯ ✯ ✯ ✯ ✯ ✯

sanctimoniously – *self-righteously*

✯ ✯ ✯ ✯ ✯ ✯ ✯ ✯ ✯ ✯

"Well, your father and I seem to have different definitions of rude," the queen said.

The king was about to yell in response when Luke said, "Count to three." When his father hesitated, Luke began counting for him. "One …two… three. Okay, now you can answer."

After a deep breath, the king said, "A rude letter proclaiming my superiority and authority over the other galaxies was sent with my signature. But I did not write it. Like your mother, the other kings don't believe that I didn't send the letters. Now intergalactic relations are at an all-time low."

"The Gremlin sent them?" Kirk asked.

"I'm sure of it," the king responded.

"Oh, dear," the queen said. "I feel terrible. I wasn't a good listener, and I didn't support you when you needed it most. I'm so sorry. Please forgive me."

"Forgiven," the king said. He smiled at the queen to convince her that he meant it.

"What can you do to improve your relationship with the other kings?" Ellen asked.

"I honestly don't know. They won't take my calls. They believe I'm a power-hungry **narcissist**."

"Oh, dear, you are neither of those things. A little hot-tempered maybe, but you're a softie at heart," the queen said

✦ ✦ ✦ ✦ ✦ ✦ ✦ ✦ ✦ ✦

narcissist – *self-centered person*

wryly – *humorously*

✦ ✦ ✦ ✦ ✦ ✦ ✦ ✦ ✦ ✦

warmly. The family sat quietly thinking for a moment when she interrupted the silence. "I have an idea."

"Oh, boy. That usually means a lot of work for us," Luke said **wryly**.

The queen ignored him. "Remember when we finished reading *Island of the Blue Dolphins* as our read aloud? Ellen, you said you wished it wasn't over."

"Yes! I'm still sad we're done with the book," Ellen answered.

"I think it's the key to creating peace in the universe again," the queen said, eyes shining.

"We're going to reread *Island of the Blue Dolphins* to keep the universe from war?" Luke asked incredulously.

It was the queen's turn to sigh. "No, Luke. After dinner, we'll go to the library and I'll explain."

Later, the family gathered in the castle library. The queen removed *The Guide to Grammar Galaxy* and opened to the article on literature unit studies. She read it aloud.

Literature Unit Studies

A literature or novel unit study is multi-subject learning based on a book or series of books. This in-depth study can make learning more satisfying. Subjects typically included in a literature unit study are language arts, history, geography, science, and art.

A unit study of a novel may begin by reading one or more chapters of a book and then completing related activities. Language arts exercises may include learning new vocabulary, discussing theme, and doing an author study. History study may include reading nonfiction books and listening to music related to the time period of the book. Geography study may include learning more about the setting of the book and its cultural traditions like foods eaten. Science may include learning more about the animals, weather, or technology mentioned in the story. Art lessons may include painting a scene from the book, drawing the characters, or imitating the art style used in the book's illustrations.

"So, a literature unit study means learning more about other subjects that are related to a book?" Luke asked.

"Precisely," the queen answered.

"We can learn more about dolphins!" Ellen said, grinning. "Could we take a trip to swim with them? That would be the best experience ever!" she said pleadingly to her father.

"That would be cool," Luke admitted. "But I don't see how a literature unit study can create peace in the universe."

"I think I do," Kirk said. "If we suggest that the galaxies work together to get kids learning…" he began.

"And we get the guardians completing a mission…" Ellen continued.

"We'll all be happily working on a shared goal," the queen said.

"There's just one problem," the king said. "The other kings are too upset with me to take my call."

"Leave that to me," the queen said, winking. "I'm in an online group with the other queens. But you children need to let the guardians know they have a mission."

Chapter 1: Literature Unit Study

Kirk, Luke, and Ellen agreed and sent the guardians a mission called Literature Unit Studies.

What does *wryly* mean?

What are some subjects that students learn about when doing a literature unit study?

Why were the other kings mad at the king of Grammar Galaxy?

Chapter 2

The queen found Ellen in her bedchamber one Saturday morning. Ellen was sitting on her bed, using her communicator to chat with a friend. The queen was aghast when she saw the state of her room. There were clothes, books, and even empty snack wrappers covering the floor.

"Young lady, you'll have to stop chatting and clean this room immediately," she stated emphatically.

Ellen sighed and rolled her eyes. "I'm not the maid," she said.

The queen was shocked by what she'd heard. "What did you just say?" she asked her daughter.

"I said I'm not the maid. And I'm busy," Ellen said, returning her attention to her communicator.

"Give me that," the queen said, yanking Ellen's communicator from her hand. "You will clean this room now! Furthermore, I'm going to discuss your attitude with your father. You deserve serious **sanctions** for this **infraction**."

The queen was shaking when she left the room. And Ellen's **indifference** worried her all the more. *What on English has gotten into her?* she wondered.

★ ★ ★ ★ ★ ★ ★ ★ ★ ★

sanctions – *punishment*
infraction – *offense*
indifference – *unconcern*

★ ★ ★ ★ ★ ★ ★ ★ ★ ★

Then she saw Kirk walking toward her in the hallway. The queen's countenance brightened. She could always count on her eldest to be positive. "Hi there, young man. What are you up to this morning?" she asked.

"Nothing," Kirk said, sighing.

"Nothing?" the queen asked. "Aren't you feeling well? That's not like you."

"Mother, I'm fine," Kirk said. "I don't always have to be doing something, do I?" he snapped. He glared at her, then walked to his own bedchamber and closed the door firmly.

The queen's eyes filled with tears. Then Luke opened his bedchamber door and looked down the hallway toward the queen. When he spotted her, he quickly closed the door.

"Not my baby, too!" the queen wailed. She ran to find her husband, weeping on the way.

She found the king in his study, leaning back in his recliner. Without waiting for him to speak, she told him what had happened with the three children. "I've failed as a mother!" she said, sobbing into her hands. After several moments, she looked up at the king, surprised that he hadn't said anything. He hadn't tried to comfort her at all.

"Don't you have anything to say?" she asked.

"Yes, I agree with you," the king said slowly.

"You agree with me?" the queen said, her voice rising. "You mean you agree that I'm a terrible mother?"

"Not necessarily," the king said.

The queen couldn't believe what she was hearing. "Not necessarily," she said in a mocking tone. "What are you saying then?"

"I'm saying it's all hopeless," he said, closing his eyes.

The queen stood watching him in shock. *It's like my family members have been replaced by aliens*, she thought. She left her husband's study, knowing that she needed time to think.

She made her way to the kitchen, hoping her friend Cook would cheer her up. The queen found her as she was getting her coat and purse. "Where are you off to?" she asked Cook as cheerfully as she could.

"I haven't had a day off in ages. Is it okay with you if I take one?" she asked in a sarcastic tone.

The queen recoiled as if she had been struck. "Of course it's okay. I'm sorry you think I wouldn't want you to have a day off," she said quietly.

Cook ignored her. Then she left the kitchen, pulling the door closed loudly behind her.

The queen was about to cry again when she stopped herself. *Something is wrong*, she thought. *It has to be the Gremlin's doing.*

She made her way to the library where she asked Screen for a status report from planet Composition.

Chapter 2: Tone & Mood

"It's always Screen this, Screen that. Never any please or thank you," Screen retorted.

The queen stuttered in surprise. "Yes…um…my apologies. Thank you for your faithful service. *Please* give me a report on planet Composition?" she said as a question.

"That's more like it," Screen responded curtly.

The queen trembled as she waited for the report.

"The only thing I see is the mood of the month is bleak and sarcastic is the tone. But NBD," Screen said.

"NBD?" the queen asked tentatively.

"No big deal?" Screen explained impatiently.

"I didn't know there was a mood or tone of the month," the queen said.

"Of course, you didn't know. You're not big into current events, are you?" The queen ignored him and he continued. "A newly formed committee chooses the mood and tone for the whole galaxy each month."

"I see. Thank you. You've been a tremendous help," the queen said cheerfully.

"Uh-huh," Screen said dismissively.

"Mood and tone," the queen said to herself. She knew what they were in general, but she wanted more information before she took action. She found an article in *The Guide to Grammar Galaxy* and read.

Tone & Mood in Literature

Tone and mood can help the reader understand the theme or main idea of a literary work.

Tone is the author's attitude toward the characters, events, and audience. Tone is determined by the vocabulary used and the syntax or arrangement of words. Tone may be described as serious, lighthearted, sarcastic, depressed, humorous, wary, and more. Edward Lear's "There Was an Old Man Who Supposed" has a mocking, teasing tone.

There was an Old Man who supposed,
That the street door was partially closed;
But some very large rats ate his coats and his hats,
While that futile [pointless] old gentleman dozed.

Chapter 2: Tone & Mood

> **Mood is the feeling or atmosphere of a piece of literature that is most notable at its beginning.** The setting, illustrations, and vocabulary are used to create mood. Mood may be romantic, mournful, cheerful, hopeless, optimistic, playful, etc. The beginning lines of "Drowned at Sea" by Henry Kendall create a dark, depressing mood.
> Gloomy cliffs, so worn and wasted with the washing of the waves,
> Are ye [you] not like giant tombstones round those lonely ocean graves?

"I don't think there should be a mood and tone of the month," the queen said aloud. "And sarcastic and bleak are the worst choices to be featured. I'm not going to get any help from my family until I get this changed." She didn't want to rely on Screen to contact the committee either. Instead, she made her way to her husband's study to look for the necessary contact information. She was pleased to find he wasn't there.

It took some convincing, but the queen was able to get the chair of the committee to cancel the Mood and Tone of the Month program. She asked the butler to have her family meet her in the study. She was relieved when she heard no backtalk from him.

When her husband and children arrived in the office, the queen explained what had been happening and why. Ellen admitted to having a messy room but didn't remember being disrespectful. The king and the boys did not remember their bad attitudes either. But everyone apologized. The queen offered forgiveness immediately and reviewed with them what she had learned about tone and mood in the guidebook.

"I'm so glad you're my mother," Ellen said, hugging the queen.

"Us, too," Kirk said, smiling while Luke nodded.

"I'm grateful that you handled this crisis for us, dear. The whole galaxy is indebted to you," the king said.

"Yes. The whole galaxy. But not everyone knows why they were experiencing bad moods and attitudes," Ellen said, thinking aloud. "I think we should send out a mission on tone and mood."

"You're right, Ellen. We need to send it out right away. Will you put it together? I've got to find Cook and make sure we're still friends," the queen answered.

Chapter 2: Tone & Mood

What does *infraction* mean?

How is mood created in literature?

Why did the English children have bad attitudes?

Chapter 3

The king was delighted to find all three of his children reading in the castle library. "What books have you chosen?" he asked them **jauntily**.

"I'm reading *Mary Poppins*!" Ellen answered eagerly.

★ ★ ★ ★ ★ ★ ★ ★ ★ ★

jauntily – *cheerfully*

★ ★ ★ ★ ★ ★ ★ ★ ★ ★

"I'm reading *Shiloh*," Luke said, smiling.

"And I'm reading *The Yearling*," Kirk answered.

"Those are excellent titles," the king said. "I won't interrupt you." He patted Kirk on the shoulder and left the library.

In the sunroom, he found the queen using her tablet. "Do you know all three of our children are reading this morning, and it isn't even raining?" he told her.

"I'm not surprised," the queen murmured in response. "They love reading."

"Yes, they do. Why shouldn't they? Reading is so **gratifying**."

18

The queen nodded **absent-mindedly**.

"What are you reading, dear?" the king asked.

The queen looked up, shamefaced. "I'm reading—, I'm looking at home decorating ideas."

"I see," the king said, frowning at her. He paused, then announced he was going to go read the book he'd checked out from the library.

When he left, the queen kept trying to enjoy her pictures. But she felt too guilty. She went to her bedchamber where she had left a new mystery novel. Once she'd started it, she was almost glad her husband had made her feel guilty.

★ ★ ★ ★ ★ ★ ★ ★ ★ ★

gratifying – *rewarding*

absent-mindedly – *distractedly*

★ ★ ★ ★ ★ ★ ★ ★ ★ ★

At dinner that evening, the king asked about the family's progress with their books.

"I'm done with mine!" Luke announced proudly.

"You read that quickly, Luke. What did you think of it?" his father asked.

"I loved it. I would do anything to protect Comet."

"I'm sure you would," the king said, smiling.

"I'm done, too!" Ellen said.

"You children are fast readers," the king commended them.

"It wasn't a very long book, though," Ellen admitted.

"It's over 200 pages, isn't it? That's a lot to read," the king continued.

"I don't think my book was that long," Ellen said.

"Did you read the print version or the ebook?" the queen asked. When Ellen said she had read the ebook, the queen said that the mystery was solved. "The ebook version always seems shorter to me."

"How about you, Kirk? How far along are you in *The Yearling*?" the king asked.

"I'm finished," Kirk said. "And I have to say it seemed quite short. Like the exposition and climax and falling action all occurred within a few pages."

"I love it when books are like that," the queen said dreamily. "It's like a fantastic trip that seems to end too soon."

"I know what you mean, Mother, but this book really did seem to end too soon," Kirk explained.

"Hm. Come to think of it, my new mystery book was very short. I guess I've become such a fast reader and mystery solver that the time just flies," she said. She noticed the king wasn't eating his dessert. "What is it, dear?" she asked.

"Today I started what I thought was a new book in a series. But the book just had several short stories in it. Something is wrong." He asked Screen for a report from planet Composition.

"Your Majesty, the only news I have from the planet is on the new Short Story Statute," Screen said.

"What Short Story Statute? I haven't been informed of this!"

"An expert on attention testified before Parliament. She shared evidence that attention spans have decreased significantly."

Screen produced a video of the woman speaking. "My recommendation is that novel-length books be adapted to the short-story format. We will have more kids reading short stories as a result. And isn't that our goal?" she implored.

"Attention spans *are* shorter," the queen said, agreeing with her.

"That may be, but the answer is not to change the very books that are likely to increase those attention spans," the king said angrily. He noted the queen's hurt look and apologized for being short with her.

"Many hours have gone into creating abridged versions of popular novels," Screen informed them.

"I've read abridged books before and I like them!" Luke interjected.

"Shortened forms of novels for young readers are a good thing, Luke. But turning novels into short stories is not. There's a difference. I would like the three of you to go to the castle library and look up short stories in *The Guide to Grammar Galaxy*. Meanwhile, I'll be talking to the Prime Minister about this terrible statute."

The queen accompanied her children to the library and read the article on short stories to them.

Short Stories

A short story is prose fiction that can be read in one sitting. There are no firm guidelines for length, but typically short stories have word counts from 1,000-4,000 words. They are often organized into collections to create a full-length book.

In short stories, less time is spent developing the plot (problem/solution) and more time is spent developing a particular mood (emotion). These stories may

> not easily be categorized into a particular genre.
>
>   Short stories have a long history, beginning in oral storytelling, folk tales, legends, and myths. But they gained new popularity in the 1800s. Some famous short stories include "The Gift of the Magi" by O. Henry, "Rip Van Winkle" by Washington Irving, and "The Tell-Tale Heart" by Edgar Allen Poe.
>
>   **Novellas** are longer than short stories, having up to 40,000 words. Some novellas are full-length novels that have been adapted for children.

"Those famous short stories sound interesting," Ellen said.

"They're wonderful stories, Ellen," the queen agreed. "Though I'm sure the Gremlin was behind the Short Story Statute, he may have done us a favor."

"What do you mean, Mother?" Kirk asked.

"Short stories aren't as popular as they once were. We could turn the Short Story Statute into Short Story Spotlight. Let's get the guardians on board with reading real short stories."

"I love that idea!" Ellen exclaimed.

"What will we do about the novels that have been turned into short stories?" Luke asked.

"I think you could make identifying true short stories part of the mission for the guardians."

The English children agreed. They worked with their mother to create a mission called Short Stories. They were excited to tell their father about their idea when he joined them in the library.

What does *gratifying* mean?

Why were the books the English family read so short?

In short stories, less time is spent on developing what?

Chapter 4

Luke found his father in the media room. He was watching the evening news before dinner.

"What's the big news?" Luke asked.

"Nothing new," the king answered. "They are discussing the anniversary of the day that will live in infamy."

"What's 'infamy' mean?"

"It's well known for being a bad day."

"But you've always said it's our choice whether it's a bad day or not."

The king smiled. "Indeed, I do say that because it's true. But on this day in history, many Americans died in an attack of the U.S. Navy. It **engaged** the country in World War II."

★ ★ ★ ★ ★ ★ ★ ★ ★ ★

engaged – *involved*

★ ★ ★ ★ ★ ★ ★ ★ ★ ★

"I didn't know about that," Luke answered thoughtfully. "That was infamy."

The king chuckled. "We had better get ready for dinner. You know how your mother is when we're late."

Luke grinned and went to wash up.

At the dinner table, Luke was chastised for having his communicator out. "I shouldn't have to remind you," the queen said.

"But it's his precious," Ellen said, pretending to cradle a communicator in her hands.

The queen hushed her.

"What's that mean, Ellen?" Luke asked.

"I'm sorry for teasing you," she said with sincerity.

"Thanks. But what does that mean, 'my precious'?" Luke responded.

"Precious means it's really valuable to you," Ellen said.

Chapter 4: Allusions

"I know what precious means," Luke said, getting exasperated. "Why did you say it that way?"

"You mean why did I say it like Gollum of *Lord of the Rings*?"

"That's where it's from?"

"Yes, of course!" Ellen answered.

"Now I understand," Kirk said.

"Now you understand what 'my precious' means?" the king asked Kirk.

"No, I know that line. Of course! What I mean is I understand why a member of Parliament asked us to support an anti-allusion act," Kirk said.

"Asked who?" the king said, suddenly concerned.

"He asked the Grammar Guys to support it."

"What's an allusion?" Luke asked.

The king ignored the question and began **ruminating** aloud, "An anti-allusion act. Of all the ridiculous ideas! Why do we need this act?"

"He said it keeps people with fewer **cultural** experiences from being left out of the conversation," Kirk answered.

★ ★ ★ ★ ★ ★ ★ ★ ★ ★

ruminating – *pondering*
cultural – *social*

★ ★ ★ ★ ★ ★ ★ ★ ★ ★

"I don't know what you're talking about," Luke said.

"I must admit I'm confused too," the queen added.

"So what will the act do?" the king continued to probe.

"Remove all allusions from books," Kirk said.

The king was aghast. "You're kidding."

"No. He said it would help us communicate better as a planet."

"I still don't know what an allusion is," Luke said, shrugging.

The king sighed. He asked that *The Guide to Grammar Galaxy* be brought to him. When it arrived, he opened the book to an article on allusions and read aloud.

Allusions
An allusion is a figure of speech that indirectly refers to books, movies, people, or events. As figures of speech, allusions are not understood literally. Allusions require knowledge of the reference to be understood.

Chapter 4: Allusions

> For example, in crossing the threshold of a new home, a father might say, "One small step for man, one giant leap for our family." The allusion is to Neil Armstrong's words when walking on the moon for the first time. The family was not literally making a giant leap into the new house but was experiencing a big change.
>
> Effective allusions are widely known and indirect. If, in the example, the father had said, "I am like Neil Armstrong taking a small step that's a giant leap for our family," the statement would be considered a **reference** rather than an allusion.

"That's one small article for Father but one giant problem for Parliament," Luke joked.

"I don't think the humor works, but you're right that we have a problem if Parliament keeps pushing an anti-allusion act," the king said.

"Why?" Ellen asked. "If there are allusions in literature that many people don't understand, maybe we should take them out," Ellen said.

The king smiled at his daughter. "Should we remove everything from books that we don't know or understand?" he asked her.

"Well, no. That wouldn't be a good idea."

"Precisely. Sometimes we read or hear allusions that we don't know. How should we respond?"

"Ask. Look it up," Kirk answered.

"Exactly, Kirk. That is how we learn. We may be inspired to read a book, watch a movie, or study history," the king said.

His children nodded.

"What are we going to do now?" Kirk asked.

"First, I'd like you three to create a mission on allusions. Then I'd like you to ask the guardians to write a letter to Parliament urging them to keep allusions in place."

Luke joked, "That's one small request from Father but one giant task for us." Everyone groaned but got to work on a mission called Allusions.

Chapter 4: Allusions

What does *ruminating* mean?

What is an allusion?

Why did the member of Parliament want allusions removed from books?

Chapter 5

The English children were excited about the Annual Poetry Reading Festival that evening. Luke was proud that he was prepared.

"I've practiced and practiced," he crowed.

"It's true," the queen said. "He is going to do a wonderful reading." Luke beamed at his mother's compliment.

"What are you reading, Luke?" the king asked, slightly embarrassed that he didn't know.

"I'm reading 'Casey at the Bat.'"

Chapter 5: Narrative Poems

"I love that poem! I can't wait to hear it," the king said. "What are you reading, Kirk?" he asked.

"I'm keeping my reading a secret," Kirk said, smiling.

"But you've rehearsed, haven't you?" the king asked, a worried frown on his face.

"Definitely!" Kirk answered.

"All right. Then we will be surprised," the king said with a relieved smile.

"Yes, and that will be nice for a change. By the time I've heard the children's practice readings, I could give them all by memory," the queen **quipped**.

The rest of the family laughed.

★ ★ ★ ★ ★ ★ ★ ★ ★ ★

quipped – *joked*
halfhearted – *unenthusiastic*

★ ★ ★ ★ ★ ★ ★ ★ ★ ★

"Ellen hasn't told me what she's reading, either," the queen told her husband.

"You're surprising us, too?" the king asked.

"Yes, I'm reading an old poem this year, and I know you're going to love it," Ellen said, hugging her father.

"I have no doubt," the king said, hugging her back.

Later at the festival, Ellen was the first of the English children to read her poem. She walked to the podium and stated the title and author. "'April Showers' by Louis Silvers and B. G. Desylva.

Life IS not a highway strewn WITH flowers
Still IT holds a goodly share OF bliss
When THE sun gives way TO April showers
Here IS the point you SHOULD never miss.

THOUGH April showers MAY come your way
They bring THE flowers THAT bloom in May
So if IT'S raining HAVE no regrets
Because IT isn't raining rain YOU know, IT'S raining violets.
AND where you see clouds upon THE hills
YOU soon will see crowds OF daffodils
SO keep on looking for A blue bird
And list'ning for HIS song
WHENever April showers come along."

27

The king and queen shared puzzled looks as the crowd gave **halfhearted** applause.

"She was emphasizing the wrong beats," the queen said.

"I know," the king agreed.

"I should have made her practice with me," the queen said.

"Indeed," the king answered, then noticed his wife's crestfallen look. "Ah well, it's a learning experience for her," he said with an encouraging smile. "That poem seems familiar to me somehow." He thought for a moment and then began humming. "It's a song! That's an old song. I don't think it works well as a poetry reading. That's the main problem, dear. It wasn't her lack of practice. But we do need to check our children's choices next time."

"Yes, we do," the queen agreed.

The two half-listened to the other readings, waiting intently for Kirk's reading. They were interested to see what their technology-obsessed boy would choose as his poem.

Kirk stepped up to the podium. "'The Rime of the Ancient Mariner' by Samuel Taylor Coleridge," he announced.

"Oh, no," the king said, his eyes wide. "We'll be here all night."

"Dear, he is our son. We can spend a few minutes listening to him read poetry," the queen said firmly.

"A few minutes would be fine. I'm worried it will be a few hours!"

"You're being impatient. It's not one of your best qualities," the queen chastised.

The king sighed and listened.

"It is an ANCIENT Mariner
And HE stoppeth one of three,
'By THY long grey beard AND glittering eye,
NOW wherefore STOPP'ST thou me?

The bridegroom's doors ARE opened wide,
And I AM next of kin;
The guests ARE met, the feast is set;
May'st hear THE merry din.'

"This isn't right," the king said, trying to get his wife's attention.

"You've said that, but what's done is done," the queen said, shrugging him off.

"No, I mean he's putting the emphasis on the wrong beats."

"Right. And it's my fault for not practicing with him," the queen said sharply.

"I'm sure that would have helped, but..." He hesitated when the queen glared at him. "I just mean that he isn't reading it correctly."

"I know what you mean," the queen retorted.

"Oh, dear, I'm sorry. I'm not blaming you. I should have checked what the children were reading and worked with them. It's my fault. Will you forgive me?"

The queen hesitated. "I thought it was a good thing that the children wanted to choose their poems. Now I know it wasn't. I do blame myself, but yes, I'll accept your apology." She kissed her husband on the cheek. She turned her attention back to Kirk's reading.

As Kirk continued to read line upon line, the king grew increasingly agitated. He knew what the rest of the parents had to be thinking. It's what *he* was thinking! He was about to contact someone to end Kirk's reading when the emcee joined Kirk at the podium.

"Kirk, this has been wonderful. Thank you so much for sharing this poem with us! But because of time limits, we are going to have to wait to hear the rest of it next year. Let's give Kirk a round of applause for this delightful reading!" he said, alternately clapping and pushing Kirk toward stage right.

"Oh, thank goodness!" the king said.

The queen thought to correct him, but she was just as happy Kirk was done. "Next up is Luke and I know his reading will be perfect. He's worked so hard," she said.

"I know it will be with you as his coach," the king said, pulling his wife close.

The two listened to many more readings before it was Luke's turn. Luke approached the podium confidently. "'Casey at the Bat' by Ernest Lawrence Thayer."

The king smiled proudly at his wife.

"The outLOOK wasn't brilliant FOR the Mudville nine THAT day:

The score STOOD four to two, with but ONE inning more to play,
And then when COONEY died at first, AND Barrows did the same,
A **pall**-like silence fell upon THE patrons of the game."

★ ★ ★ ★ ★ ★ ★ ★ ★

pall – *gloom*

★ ★ ★ ★ ★ ★ ★ ★ ★

"He's not reading it right," the king said hesitantly. He didn't want to make his wife angry.

"I know! I don't understand it. That isn't how he read it in practice at all," the queen said. She hesitated. "Do you think the Gremlin could be up to something?"

"Yes, and I can't believe I didn't think of it sooner," the king said. "As soon as Luke is done, let's get the children home. We have to determine what's happening."

The couple made their way backstage to find their three children. They told them and the stage manager that an urgent matter required them to leave early.

On the way home, the royal couple explained that the children hadn't been reading their poems correctly. Though the three were disappointed, they were as eager as their parents to learn what the Gremlin had done to cause the problem.

At the castle, the king had everyone follow him to their library. Once there, he directed Screen to give him a status report on Poetry City.

"The only noteworthy item I have is a new poetry conductor." Screen played a video clip of the conductor pointing to particular words and syllables with his baton to emphasize them.

"Those beats shouldn't be emphasized in that poem, should they, dear?" the queen asked.

"No. Now I know why you weren't reading correctly. Come to think of it, the other children's readings were wrong as well! I was so focused on my own children that I missed the signs. We could have acted much sooner. Forgive me!" the king asked his children.

Kirk, Luke, and Ellen quickly assured him of their forgiveness.

"I need to have that conductor replaced immediately. But I want you to review how to read poems with rhythm. I'm going to read from *The Guide to Grammar Galaxy*."

> ### Reading Poems with Rhythm & Rhyme
>
> **To read rhyming poetry, first identify rhyming words at the end of lines.** Two lines that contain rhyming words in a stanza (a poem's paragraph) are called a **couplet**. Three rhyming lines are called a **triplet**.
>
> Lines in a couplet or triplet should be read with the same rhythm or beat to allow the rhyming words to be emphasized. The following lines from "Annabel Lee" by Edgar Allen Poe show the emphasized beats in this triplet stanza:
>
> It was MANy and MANy a YEAR aGO, in a KINGdom BY the **SEA**,
> That a MAIDen there LIVED whom YOU may KNOW by the NAME of ANNabell **LEE**;
> And this MAIDen she LIVED with NO other THOUGHT than to LOVE and BE loved by **ME**.
> Clapping as you read can help you keep the rhythm of the poem.

When the king finished reading, he said, "That reminds me. Every one of you chose a narrative poem this year."

"What's a narrative poem?" Luke asked.

"I'm glad you asked," the king said, smiling. He opened the guidebook to an article on narrative poems.

> ### Narrative Poems
>
> **Narrative poems tell stories in verses and often use rhythm and rhyme.** These stories, which have characters, plot, and a setting, are often told by a single narrator or speaker.
>
> Narrative poetry has a long history. The rhythm and rhyme of narrative poems made stories easier to memorize and share before there was a way to write them down.
>
> **Epics are long, narrative poems written about heroes or gods.** The *Iliad* and the *Odyssey* by Homer are famous epic poems about the Trojan War.
>
> **Ballads are short, narrative poems often set to music because of their predictable rhythm.** Folk songs are a form of ballad.

"Ellen, your poem 'April Showers' is a song. When we have handled the crisis in Poetry City, I will find it for you and play it," the king said.

"It's funny that we all chose narrative poems to read," Luke said.

"But it's not funny that the conductor in Poetry City has us reading them with the wrong rhythm," Kirk said.

"Kirk, I have to tell you that even with the right emphasis, no one wants to listen to 'Rime of the Ancient Mariner' in its entirety," the king said.

Kirk shrugged, feeling a little embarrassed.

"I think we should send out a mission on narrative poetry," Ellen said. "That way, no matter who the new conductor is, we'll know how to read poetry correctly."

"Splendid idea, Ellen. I'm going to handle the conductor while you three write the mission on narrative poems."

What does *halfhearted* mean?

What is a ballad?

Why were the English children reading their poems with the wrong rhythm?

Chapter 6

"Are you feeling prepared for the Galactic Aptitude Test?" the king asked his children at dinner. "How are your practice test scores?"

Kirk, Luke, and Ellen shrugged.

"What is the hesitation?" the king asked.

"It's the reading section," Luke groaned. His brother and sister nodded.

"But you're all good readers. That should be the easiest part," the king said.

"It should be," Kirk agreed. "But it isn't."

The king was irritated at the thought of his children not doing well on a reading test. "There's a simple fix for this: more reading. You three need to read instead of doing other things. Until exam day, there will be no gaming or watching shows," he pronounced.

"But what about *Lost in Space*? The premier is tonight. We can still watch it, can't we?" Ellen pleaded.

"I'm afraid not, Ellen," the king said firmly.

The queen looked as disappointed as the children. "They already read a lot, dear," she began on their behalf.

"I've made up my mind," the king said. "My children will score well in reading." He dismissed the children to their rooms to read.

The kids agreed, knowing it was no use arguing.

A few days later at breakfast, the king asked the children if their practice test scores were improving. "No," they admitted.

"And I've been reading a lot!" Luke said defensively.

"Well, keep it up. We have to see improvement," the king said, frowning.

"The readings are so boring!" Luke complained.

"And they don't even make sense," Ellen agreed.

"One article I read was about the history of women's fashion," Kirk groaned.

Chapter 6: Nonfiction Reading Comprehension

"Reading is reading," the king said tersely. "We can learn from all of it. I'll hear no more complaining about it."

That evening as the king and queen got ready for bed, the queen suggested that the ban on nonreading activities be lifted. "The children have been reading whenever they can. I think they've earned a break, don't you?" the queen asked.

"Not until the test scores come up. Our children are leading the way. If kids don't understand what they're reading, the future is **dismal**."

★ ★ ★ ★ ★ ★ ★ ★ ★ ★

dismal – *depressing*
comprehend – *understand*
primes – *prepares*

★ ★ ★ ★ ★ ★ ★ ★ ★ ★

The queen nodded and was ready to say more when she thought better of it. The king quickly fell asleep while she kept thinking about the children's reading scores. She knew they could read and **comprehend** well, so why were they struggling?

She couldn't sleep, so she decided to go to the castle library. Comet yawned and followed her. He curled up on a chair and snoozed while she looked through the table of contents for *The Guide to Grammar Galaxy*. "Reading Comprehension," she said aloud. She skimmed the article and found the subtitle Nonfiction Reading Comprehension.

Nonfiction Reading Comprehension

Nonfiction text can be wordy or dry. To improve comprehension of the material, begin by skimming the title and a short section of text. Glance at subtitles and any images or graphs. Ask yourself what the article or chapter is about. Preparing to read nonfiction in this way **primes** your mind to make connections with other information you've learned.

Next, ask yourself what you already know about the subject. For example, in reading about the preservation of moon rocks, you may recall watching a documentary about the moon landing.

Then, ask yourself what personal experience you have with the subject matter. For the moon rocks article, you may remember touching a moon rock on display at a science center. Or, you may recall the last time you saw a full moon. You marveled at how close it looked.

Finally, consider the importance of the information for your life or the world. The

Chapter 6: Nonfiction Reading Comprehension

> article on moon rocks mentions a future mission to the moon. Do you think there will there be controversy about another moon mission? Perhaps someone your age will go. Would you be brave enough to volunteer?
>
> Considering these connections to the material will you help you focus on the reading, understand it better, and remember more of it.

"That's it!" the queen said. "I know how to help the children with their reading scores." She smiled, a little proud of herself, and made her way to her bedchamber. She suddenly felt very tired.

The next morning, she had the guidebook at the breakfast table. "I have a question for you," she said to the children. "Do you find the reading passages on the GAT interesting?"

"I'll answer that one," Luke blurted out. "No!"

Kirk and Ellen laughed. "I have to agree with Luke on this one," Kirk said.

"Me, too," Ellen agreed.

"Perfect," the queen answered.

"How is it perfect that they think the reading is boring?" the king asked, frowning.

"Because I have the solution to it." The queen read them the passage from the guidebook about nonfiction reading comprehension. Then she summarized it.

"Look over the passage before you begin reading it. Read the title and subtitles. Pay attention to any images or graphs. Ask yourself what the reading is about. Then ask yourself if you have any experience with the topic—personal experience or other knowledge. Then find a way to make the reading relevant. If you can decide why it's important to know for your life or our galaxy, you'll understand it and remember it."

"So, I can remember what you read to us by thinking about improving my test score?" Luke asked.

"Precisely," the queen said.

"I have another idea for making a connection," Ellen said. "The guardians need a mission on nonfiction reading comprehension."

"Great idea, Ellen!" Kirk said.

"Splendid!" the king agreed.

Chapter 6: Nonfiction Reading Comprehension

"Here's another idea. Could you lift the ban on games and shows?" Luke said.

The king laughed. "I believe I can."

What does *primes* mean?

What is the first step in nonfiction reading comprehension?

Why did the king ban games and shows?

Chapter 7

The queen was so excited about her announcement that she could hardly control herself. "We have a special treat for you children. We are going camping!"

"Camping?" they responded excitedly.

"Yes, camping. I finally talked your mother into it by agreeing to rent an RV. That's an acronym for recreational vehicle," the king said.

"Yes, and it's a beautiful RV with every **convenient** feature," the queen added.

★ ★ ★ ★ ★ ★ ★ ★ ★ ★

convenient – *helpful*

★ ★ ★ ★ ★ ★ ★ ★ ★ ★

"Is Cook coming with us?" Ellen asked.

"No, I'm going to be cooking," the queen answered.

"And I'll be barbecuing," the king added.

The children seemed concerned.

"Don't you worry. We have been collecting some tried-and-true recipes," the queen said proudly.

"Is Cook going to practice with you before we go?" Ellen asked hesitantly.

"No, I haven't asked her to help. But I suppose I could," the queen said, considering. She tried not to take offense to Ellen's suggestion.

That weekend, the children were **exuberant** as they headed to the campground in the RV.

★ ★ ★ ★ ★ ★ ★ ★ ★

exuberant – *enthusiastic*

★ ★ ★ ★ ★ ★ ★ ★ ★

"Do we have what we need to make s'mores?" Luke asked.

"Indeed, we do," the queen answered cheerily.

"Don't worry, Mother. I know how to make them. We made them at Ryan's house," he said.

"All right. I won't worry," she said, smiling.

With some impatience and confusion, the king managed to get the RV hooked up at their campsite. When he finished, he announced that the family would be going for a hike.

They hiked along a creek, taking time to dip in the water when they felt too warm. The queen pointed out unique plants and wildlife as they walked.

That evening, the boys helped their father build a campfire. They were proud of their accomplishment. Ellen and the queen handed them the foil-wrapped sandwiches that Cook had insisted on preparing. Later, the family declared them delicious and perfectly toasted.

For dessert, they had fun roasting their marshmallows and adding them to graham crackers and chocolate. Ellen was enjoying hers when she got a message on her communicator.

Ellen read the message and gasped.

"What is it? Is something wrong?" the queen asked.

"Yes. No. I want to go home," Ellen said frantically.

"What on English? What was the message you got?" the king asked.

"It's, it's, we're not safe," Ellen stammered.

"Why aren't we safe, dear?" the queen asked in a soothing voice.

Ellen wondered if telling her family would do more harm than good. But she decided to be honest. "Because of the spiders," she said.

"What?" Luke exclaimed, laughing. "Because of spiders? You're afraid of spiders, so we have to go home?"

The queen hushed him. "What did you read that has you so frightened of spiders?" she asked her daughter.

Ellen reluctantly handed her mother the communicator. The queen read the message and tried not to laugh. But Ellen noticed. "How can you think that's funny?" Ellen wailed, running to the RV.

"Girls," Luke said to Kirk with an eye roll.

"What did the message say?" the king asked.

"It was a story about a girl who went camping and was bitten on the cheek by a spider. Weeks later, baby spiders hatched from her cheek."

"Ack," Luke said. "That's gross. No wonder Ellen is scared."

"Perhaps it is wise for us to leave," Kirk said. "There are quite a few spiders here," he said, surveying the ground warily.

The king laughed. "Kirk, the message Ellen received is what is called an urban legend." Before Kirk could ask more, he asked his wife to call Ellen back outside. While she did, the king used his communicator to produce an article on urban legends. He read it for the family.

Urban Legends

Urban legends are scary or funny fictional stories presented as true tales. Urban legends, also called urban myths, are spread orally and in written form. These stories often arise out of a combination of fear and lack of information.

The tale usually involves a friend or a friend of a friend. Thus, determining if the story is true is more difficult. The stories are often changed as they are spread to include local details, making them more believable. The stories often have a moral or warning.

Urban legends may be based on actual events or are at least **plausible**. Urban legends, once spread, can be difficult to disprove. Consult a website that fact checks these stories before sharing them.

"So, you're saying it's not true that spiders hatched out of that girl's cheek? My friend said it happened to her friend's friend." Ellen said.

★★★★★★★★★★

plausible – *believable*

★★★★★★★★★★

"That's what I'm saying, my dear," the king said.

"I'm still afraid that could happen to me," Ellen said, shuddering.

The king used his communicator to fact check the story. In a moment he read aloud. "Spiders cannot lay eggs inside or live inside the skin or *any part of the human body*," he said with emphasis.

Ellen looked hopeful for a moment. Then she said, "Maybe the Gremlin wants us to *think* that spiders don't lay eggs inside us when they actually *do*."

The king sighed but replied patiently. "Ellen, the Gremlin's goal is to destroy the English language. He isn't known for being an insect terrorist."

Ellen giggled nervously at first. Then the family joined her in real laughter.

"There's one thing that still bothers me," Ellen said.

"Ticks?" Luke suggested mischievously.

"No," Ellen said, scowling. "It's urban legends. My friends send me stories like this a lot. I don't think they know that they're not true."

"You make an excellent point, Ellen. I know we're camping, but I think you three should send a mission to the guardians on urban legends," the king said.

The English children agreed. They used their communicators to put together a mission before they turned in for the night.

What does *plausible* mean?

Why did Ellen want to leave the campground early?

Why do you think urban legends are hard to disprove?

Chapter 8

The king asked his children what they were reading. They were in the sunroom with him and his wife, and each had a book.

"I'm reading *My Friend Flicka*," Ellen said, returning her attention to the book.

"Another horse book," the queen said, smiling.

"I'm reading *Johnny Tremain*," Kirk replied.

"You like historical fiction, don't you, Kirk?" the king asked.

Kirk nodded and returned to reading.

Luke said nothing.

"Luke, what about you?" the king **prodded**.

"I'm reading this book and I don't understand it. I'm not good at reading. I don't even like to read!" Luke said, angrily tossing the book. He bolted from the room before his parents could respond.

"My word! What has gotten into him?" the queen asked aloud.

"I don't know, but I'll not have a son who doesn't like to read!" the king said, his voice rising.

"Dear, I'm sure he didn't mean it," the queen said to placate him.

"Perhaps words are missing from his book," Kirk suggested. "The Gremlin could be up to his old tricks."

"I haven't seen any missing words in my book. What about you, Kirk?" Ellen asked.

"Well, no. The words all seem to be here."

"I haven't noticed any missing words in my book. Have you, dear?" the queen asked.

"No. All the more reason to think that Luke has decided he doesn't like to read," the king said.

"I can't believe that. Luke loves to read," the queen said.

"He does, but sometimes it's hard for him. I know I don't like to do hard things," Ellen said.

★ ★ ★ ★ ★ ★ ★ ★ ★ ★

prodded – *urged*

★ ★ ★ ★ ★ ★ ★ ★ ★ ★

Chapter 8: Shakespeare

"Hm. We could review his phonics, and I can make sure that he knows the new vocabulary words before he starts reading," the queen said.

"I'm surprised you haven't been doing that already," the king said.

The queen's eyes blazed. "If you thought it was important, you certainly could have been working with him."

The king realized his mistake. "You are right, dear. I could have been working with him on his reading," he said apologetically.

The queen's countenance softened to the king's relief.

Kirk moved to Luke's chair and picked up his book. He was smiling. "I don't think the Gremlin tampered with Luke's book. And I don't think his reading skills are weak," he said. When the rest of the family asked why, he explained. "He's reading Shakespeare's *Hamlet*." He laughed and the king and queen joined him.

"No wonder he was struggling!" the king said.

"Poor dear," the queen agreed.

"Why does that book title explain it?" Ellen asked.

"Ellen, remember when I played Romeo in *Romeo and Juliet*? The play was written by Shakespeare. I learned my lines, but half the time I didn't know what I was saying!" Kirk said.

The king and queen laughed.

"We haven't taught the children how to read and enjoy Shakespeare, have we, dear?" the king asked seriously.

"You know, I don't think we have," she answered.

"Then I have a **notion** that can change that. Why don't we declare this month Shakespeare Month? I honestly can't believe we haven't given the Bard this honor before," the king said. "Let's go give Luke the good news."

★ ★ ★ ★ ★ ★ ★ ★ ★ ★
notion – *idea*
merely – *only*
★ ★ ★ ★ ★ ★ ★ ★ ★ ★

Kirk and Ellen were surprised and looked to the queen. She **merely** shrugged and motioned for them to follow their father to Luke's bedchamber.

When they arrived, the king announced that he had good news. "I thought you didn't like to read, Luke. Now I know that you were reading Shakespeare." The rest of the family nodded kindly.

"Oh? So that explains it?" Luke asked with relief.

Chapter 8: Shakespeare

"Yes! Here's what we're going to do. We are going to devote an entire month to reading Shakespeare in this galaxy. Isn't that wonderful?" the king asked, waiting for Luke's enthusiastic response.

Luke laughed until he saw that the rest of the family wasn't. "Is this the Gremlin's idea?" he asked.

"Of course not!" the king said sharply. "It's my idea and it's a splendid one."

The queen grasped the king's arm. "Allow me, dear," she said, moving close to Luke. "What your father didn't say is that he knows we haven't taught you how to read and enjoy Shakespeare. That's what Shakespeare Month is all about. Right, dear?" she asked sweetly.

"Right," the king said, reddening a little.

"But I don't know how it's even possible to read Shakespeare!" Luke wailed, burying his head in his pillow.

The king was about to chastise him when the queen interrupted. "We need to read what the guidebook has to say about Shakespeare. Don't you agree, dear?" she asked the king.

Her husband nodded and invited the children to follow him to the castle library. There he removed *The Guide to Grammar Galaxy* from its shelf and read the article on Shakespeare aloud.

Shakespeare

William Shakespeare is often called the greatest English writer of all time. He lived in England from the late 1500s to the early 1600s. He wrote 39 plays and many poems. He was also an actor with the nickname of "the Bard."

Little is known about Shakespeare personally, which has led to theories that his works were written by someone else.

While Shakespeare's plays are written in English, some pronouns for *you* are different from what we use today. *Thou* is used as a sentence subject and *thee* is used as a direct object, indirect object, or object of the preposition.

__Thou__, like an exorcist, has conjured up my mortified spirit.
I would have had __thee__ there and here again. – Julius Caesar

There are three steps in understanding and enjoying a Shakespearean play:
1. **Read a plot synopsis.** This is a summary of what happens in the play.

Chapter 8: Shakespeare

> 2. **Watch the play in person or on film.**
> 3. **Read an annotated or adapted version of the play.** An annotated version has the original words of the play alongside easier-to-understand language. An adapted version only includes the easier-to-understand language.
> 4. **Make notes about who the characters are as you read.** This will keep you from becoming confused.
>
> The best plays to begin an adventure in Shakespeare include *A Midsummer Night's Dream*, *Twelfth Night*, and *As You Like It*.

"Luke, are you feeling any better about Shakespeare Month now?" the queen asked.

"Well, I do like the idea of watching a movie," he said hesitantly.

"Why don't we look at a plot summary of these three plays? Then we can decide which one we'll read for Shakespeare Month," Ellen suggested.

The king nodded approvingly.

"I have an idea, too," Kirk said. "I think we should send out a mission. I'm sure Luke isn't the only one who doesn't enjoy reading Shakespeare."

"I was hoping you would say that," the queen said with a smile.

The three English children began working on a mission. And even Luke was feeling excited about reading Shakespeare.

What does *merely* mean?

What is the first step in understanding a Shakespearean play?

Why was Luke struggling to enjoy *Hamlet*?

Chapter 9

"Have you read it?" Cher asked Ellen.

"Read what?" Ellen replied.

"The article about your dad."

"No," Ellen said frowning. "Where?"

"Let me see if I can find it," Cher said, using her communicator. "Here it is," she said finally. She handed it to Ellen to read.

Ellen sat down on a bench to read. Her mouth fell open in surprise, and she gasped numerous times.

"I know, right?" Cher said.

Ellen felt a discomfort she couldn't explain. She suddenly wanted to go home.

"Okay. Call me," Cher said, disappointed by the abrupt end to their time together.

Chapter 9: Satire

Ellen couldn't get home fast enough. She had to talk to Kirk. Was it true? If what they had written about their father was true, she was very, very worried.

She was breathless by the time she found Kirk in the computer lab.
"What are you so excited about? Are shoes on sale?" Kirk joked. When he saw the look on Ellen's face, he apologized. "What's going on?"
"Have you read this?" Ellen asked, searching for the article she'd read earlier. When she pulled it up on her communicator, she handed it to Kirk.
"No," Kirk murmured as he began to read. He read intently and made several quiet exclamations as he did.
"Is it true?" Ellen asked.
"I think it has to be," Kirk said solemnly.
"Why?" Ellen asked.
"This is a news site. If it isn't true, they can be sued for libel. I don't think they would take that risk."
"What's libel?"
"It's false published information that damages someone's reputation."
"Okay. If it's true, then what do we do?" Ellen asked. "Do we have Luke read it?"
Kirk sighed. "I don't know. I think Luke will be so disappointed in Father. But on the other hand, I think he has the right to know."
Ellen nodded. "Okay. Let's show him."

Luke was happy and curious to see his brother and sister at his bedchamber door. "Is Mother on one of her cleaning **binges**?" he joked.
"No, Luke, this is serious," Ellen answered soberly.

★ ★ ★ ★ ★ ★ ★ ★ ★ ★

binges – *sprees*
flabbergasted – *stunned*

★ ★ ★ ★ ★ ★ ★ ★ ★ ★

"Okay, what is it?" he asked. The two explained that a news article had been published about their father that he needed to read.
Luke read slowly and seemed **flabbergasted**. "Father is—"
"I know," Ellen said, interrupting him sympathetically.
"But how do we know it's true?" Luke asked.

46

"It's a news site," Kirk said. "They have to **verify** their facts."

"All right. What do we do then?" Luke asked. "Do we tell him we don't agree with what he's doing? We don't agree, do we?"

★ ★ ★ ★ ★ ★ ★ ★ ★ ★

verify – *confirm*

★ ★ ★ ★ ★ ★ ★ ★ ★ ★

"No. He must have a good reason, though," Ellen said.

"I say we wait until he talks to us about it," Kirk suggested. His siblings agreed this was a good plan.

At dinner that evening, the king cheerfully asked how the children had spent their Saturday. He was met with a chorus of "nothing" and blank looks. He found it odd but went on to suggest that they play a board game.

"I have schoolwork to do," Kirk said.

"Me too," Luke and Ellen said in unison.

"Schoolwork on a Saturday night?" the king asked incredulously.

When the children nodded, he shrugged and asked Cook to bring him another serving of dessert. The queen frowned but was ignored.

Later that evening as the king and queen were getting into bed, the king mentioned the children's strange behavior. "They weren't even looking at me. Don't you think that's odd, dear?"

"Mm-hm," she murmured absentmindedly as she focused on her tablet. Something she read made her more alert. She began reading intently and then laughed aloud.

"What's so funny?" the king asked.

"Oh, dear, this article about you is hilarious."

"An article about me?" he asked, hand to chest. The queen answered by handing him the tablet to read for himself.

The king chuckled soon after reading. "I've had automatic grammar checkers installed in people's homes. I call the program Big Grammar," he said, guffawing. "And I personally review the worst errors." His belly was quaking with laughter as he continued reading.

"Even his own children are watched," he read aloud. He started to laugh, then stopped. "You don't suppose the children have read this article and thought it was true?" he asked.

"Oh, dear," the queen said with concern.

"That would explain their odd behavior," he said.

"It would," the queen agreed.

The two decided to talk with them about the article the next day.

Ellen's face blanched when the king mentioned the article to the three of them at breakfast. She tremulously admitted that they had read it. "We don't understand why you would start Big Grammar and you'd give out awful punishments like hundreds of pages of copywork, but we support you," Ellen said breathlessly.

The king tried to keep from laughing but failed. "Ellen, I have not created a Big Grammar program and I have not made anyone do hundreds of pages of copywork."

"You haven't?" Ellen asked, her eyes welling up with tears. "Oh, Father," she said, getting up to embrace him tightly.

The king hugged Ellen back and smiled at the boys. "I don't believe I have taught the three of you about satire."

He asked the butler to get *The Guide to Grammar Galaxy* from the castle library for him. When it arrived, he read the entry on satire aloud to them.

Satire
Satire is the use of humor, irony, or exaggeration to poke fun in a good-natured way. It can also be used to criticize policies, leaders, or organizations. Satire is used by websites, cartoonists, and some talk show hosts. Sometimes satire is not recognized as such, causing the spread of misinformation and sometimes outrage. A **parody** is satire in the form of imitation. For example, the book *Goodnight iPad* by Ann Droyd is a parody of *Goodnight Moon* by Margaret Wise Brown. It pokes fun at our love of modern technology. **Diminution** is satire that makes something seem smaller than it is in size or importance. Describing political leaders as children fighting is an example of diminution. **Inflation** is exaggerating or enlarging something so that it seems ridiculous. A politician who has a noticeable nose will have an enormous nose in a satirical cartoon. **Juxtaposition** is placing items together as though they are of equal importance when they are not. For example: *What I look for as a movie critic is believable character development, a unique plot, and well-buttered popcorn.*

"So, you're saying that the article about you is satire?" Ellen asked.

"And you're not listening to our grammar all the time?" Luke added.

Chapter 9: Satire

"Right, Ellen. I haven't started a Big Grammar program, but I do listen to your grammar, Luke, with these," he said, pointing to his ears.

"Was the author making fun of the importance you place on grammar?" Kirk asked.

"Yes, Kirk. He was using inflation as a literary technique. It did make me laugh, but it won't make me back off my focus on good grammar."

The kids smiled.

"Father, Cher showed me the article about you. Other kids may believe the article is true. I think we should send a mission on satire to the guardians. Don't you?" Ellen asked.

"Absolutely! I'd like the three of you to begin work on it as soon as possible," he answered.

What does *flabbergasted* mean?

What is a parody?

Why did the English children believe the article about their father was true?

Unit II: Adventures in Spelling & Vocabulary

Chapter 10

With the science fair quickly approaching, the queen wanted to check on her children's projects. Kirk was planning a robotics demonstration. He talked in such great detail that the queen had to cut him off. She smiled at her son's enthusiasm.

Luke planned to do a two-stage rocket demonstration. He said he had seen a video of it and was happy that it was easy. The queen smiled at her fun- and leisure-loving son.

The queen found her daughter in her bedchamber reading. When Ellen heard the question about the science fair, she frowned. "Do I have to participate?" she whined.

"Yes," the queen said. "We are committed to it."

"But I'm not good at science," Ellen complained. "That's for Kirk and not for me."

"Ellen, science isn't just about robotics. It's about animals, too, and you love animals," the queen reminded her.

"We haven't learned about animals in science since I was little," Ellen replied, looking sad. "I can't do an animal report for the science fair anymore," she sighed.

"I suppose that is more for younger students," the queen agreed. "But there must be some area of science that interests you," she said.

Ellen shook her head, tears welling up in her eyes.

"Ellen, what's wrong?" the queen asked, putting her arm around her.

"Nothing," she said, wiping away a tear. "I'm just not good at science."

"I don't think that's true, dear. We will find something you're interested in."

Comet appeared at the door as if on cue. He jumped on the bed and was immediately hugged by an emotional Ellen.

The queen left the two of them and went to find the king to discuss the problem.

The king was reading the paper in the sunroom when the queen entered. He seemed distracted as she explained Ellen's insecurity with science.

"Well, science isn't the most important subject in the world. We can let her skip participating," he said.

The queen was shocked. "So, we just let her skip it?" she asked.

"Yes. I don't think it's a big deal," the king said, looking **longingly** at his newspaper.

✯ ✯ ✯ ✯ ✯ ✯ ✯ ✯ ✯ ✯

longingly – *desirously*

sputtering – *stammering*

✯ ✯ ✯ ✯ ✯ ✯ ✯ ✯ ✯ ✯

"Maybe it isn't a big deal for her to miss one science fair. But are you going to let her skip everything she isn't comfortable with?" she asked, her voice rising. Before the king could reply, she continued. "Don't you want to help her get past this problem with science? I'm surprised at you. I really am." The queen turned and left, leaving the king **sputtering**.

He sighed, realizing that he had to talk with his daughter. He didn't want her to lack confidence. And while science wasn't his favorite subject either, he knew it was important.

He found Ellen reading in bed, Comet still by her side. She quit reading but didn't smile when he came in. "Mother told you I don't want to do the science fair. You're here to convince me. Am I right?" she asked.

The king laughed. "Partly right. I'm more interested in learning why you don't like science. I prefer language arts, of course," he said, smiling. "But science is responsible for so many of the things you enjoy."

"Like what?" she asked.

The king stroked his beard thoughtfully. "Well, animals. You love animals. We wouldn't know much about them or how to care for them without science."

"Yes. But I can't do an animal report for the science fair. That's for babies."

"Right. Okay. That's one small part of science. I've got it! You like to travel. We wouldn't have any forms of transportation without science."

"That's true. But I'm not interested in rockets or trains."

Chapter 10: Science Vocabulary

"Yes. I can see that, too. Hm." He looked at his daughter's book lying on her bed. *Princess Academy*. "You like stories about royalty?" he asked. Ellen nodded. "Have you read the story about Archimedes?" Ellen shook her head.

"Hieron, the king of Syracuse, had a new gold crown made. He didn't believe that the goldsmith had used pure gold in making it. So, he asked Archimedes to prove that it wasn't pure gold."

"And did he?" she asked eagerly.

"Yes! But he had to use science to do it. He used the principle of buoyancy." Ellen frowned and the king noticed. "What's wrong?"

"I don't know what that means!"

"Buoyancy?"

"Yes. What is buoyancy? I hate science because it's not written in English!" She buried her head in her pillow and the king **suppressed** a laugh.

★ ★ ★ ★ ★ ★ ★ ★ ★ ★

suppressed – *repressed*

★ ★ ★ ★ ★ ★ ★ ★ ★ ★

"I think I'm understanding why you don't like science. And I think I know something that will help. Let's get your brothers and go to the castle library. There's something I want to show you in *The Guide to Grammar Galaxy*."

Once in the library, the king read them an article on science vocabulary.

Science Vocabulary

Latin and Classic Greek words are often used in science. This is because science textbooks were written in Latin for thousands of years. Ancient Greeks were the first to study plants, so many plant names are Greek. However, English is the language of most computer programming and aviation (flying) science.

You can learn science vocabulary by studying Greek and Latin word roots. See the chart that follows.

Other strategies for learning science vocabulary include:
-regularly reading science materials
-writing the new vocabulary word, its meaning, a picture, and a sentence with the word in your Word Book

> -playing vocabulary games with the new words
> -using the new word in conversation

Common Greek & Latin Science Word Roots			
Root	Meaning	Root	Meaning
spect	see, observe	vac	empty
hydr	water	chron	time
therm	heat	bene	good
aqu	water	dyna	power
kinesis	movement	syn	with, together
ab	move away	circ	round
duc	lead, make	gen	to birth
lev	to lift	luc, lum	light
omni	all	bio	life

"Ellen, I think learning science vocabulary will help you enjoy science more," the king said.

"I remember learning that *bio* means life. But what about the buoyancy you were talking about?" she asked. "That wasn't in the word list."

"Right. *Buoyancy* has French and Spanish origins. It means 'to float,'" he explained. "I was telling Ellen about Archimedes," he told the boys. "The story goes that he was asked to prove that a crown was not real gold. When getting into a bathtub one day, he realized that the amount of water that was displaced or moved when he got into the tub was equal to the volume of his body. In other words, he could use the principle that the buoyant or upward force on an object in water is equal to the weight of the water displaced by the object. Because gold is heavier than silver, Archimedes could measure how much water was displaced by the crown. That would let him know if it was real gold. The story is that he was so excited about this way of solving the problem that he ran down the street naked, yelling, 'Eureka! Eureka!' which means 'I've found it.' We don't know that he said it, but that's the story."

"And what did he find out about the crown?" Ellen asked eagerly.

"The crown was made using some silver. It was not solid gold," the king answered.

"Did the king have the goldsmith thrown in the dungeon?" Ellen asked.

"I bet he ordered his head cut off instead," Luke snickered.

"Luke!" Ellen chastised him.

"I don't know what happened to the goldsmith. But I can see you like this story. Ellen, I think a demonstration of Archimedes's buoyancy principle would make a great science fair exhibit, don't you?" the king said.

Ellen smiled. "Do we have a solid gold crown I can use?"

"I'm afraid not," the king laughed. "But I think we can come up with a substitute. I am just now realizing that we have something else to do besides preparing your science fair entry."

When the children asked, he explained that he wanted them to create a science vocabulary mission. The three of them began working immediately. The king thought taking a bath was a good idea.

What does *sputtering* mean?

What is one way to learn new science vocabulary words?

Why didn't Ellen want to participate in the science fair?

Chapter II

As they were preparing for bed one evening, the queen suggested they have a date night. "It's been so long since we have had a night out, just the two of us," she said pleadingly.

The king stifled a groan. "Going out can be expensive. And we have the best cook in the galaxy. Furthermore, we can see any entertainment we want right here."

Chapter 11: Oxymorons

"Not the entertainment I want to see," the queen replied. "How about this? We can have Cook make us a romantic meal alone. Then we can go and see the new comedian everyone is raving about."

"Everyone is raving about?" the king asked, frowning.

"Yes! All my friends have seen him and loved him."

"All your friends? Hm." The king started to protest, but the queen gave him her best beseeching look. "When is it?" he sighed, giving up.

"This Friday. Thank you so much!" she said, hugging him. She was nearly jumping up and down with excitement.

"You're welcome," he said warmly. "It will be nice to have a night out with you."

The night of the comedy show, the queen led her husband to the front row of seats. The king resisted. "They always pick on the people in the front row."

"I know! It will be fun. Be a good sport, dear," the queen urged him. The king sighed and sat down. "Everyone will love you for being able to laugh at yourself."

The king rolled his eyes to disagree but wondered if his wife was right.

Soon the emcee was on the stage and introduced the comedian. "Please help me welcome the little giant of comedy, Oxymoron!"

As the audience applauded, the king whispered to his wife. "His name is Oxymoron? You didn't tell me."

The queen waved him off and whistled loudly. The king was startled. "I didn't know you could do that!" he said, referring to the whistle.

"There are plenty of things you don't know about me," she said, winking.

The king was **charmed**. He tried to ignore the unease he felt because of the comedian's name.

charmed – *pleased*

"Welcome to the show, everyone!" the comedian started. "They told me backstage that we have been graced with the presence of two special guests—the king and queen of Grammar Galaxy. Everyone, please give them a round of applause," he said beginning to applaud himself.

The royal couple flushed with embarrassment.

57

Chapter 11: Oxymorons

"You obviously wanted to have a night alone together," the comedian said. "Just you and a small crowd hanging out together."

The king laughed. He wanted to say, "Exactly! Not what I had in mind for a date," but he said nothing.

"Well, we want you two to have an awful good time, right?" he asked the audience. They responded with hoots and applause.

"How long have you two been married?" he asked the king.

The king hesitated, unsettled by the attention. "Fourteen years?" he said as a question.

"That sounds like a definite maybe to me," Oxymoron teased. The king smiled ruefully.

"With him not knowing for sure how long you've been married, it's a minor miracle you're still together. Am I right?" the comedian asked the queen.

The queen nodded, laughing. The king was not happy with her response.

"But I guess if you want to be a queen, he's your only choice," he said. The queen and the rest of the audience laughed. The king reddened.

"I better be careful. This might be a working vacation for our king. I want to use terribly good grammar, or I'll suddenly be found missing." The audience laughed, but the king's mouth was set in a hard line.

"Hey, some true fiction about our king for you. I have it from a source inside the palace that the code name they use for him is Jumbo Shrimp. His super-secret code name is the Larger Half." The audience roared and the queen was holding her stomach, laughing.

The king had his arms folded across his chest. He scowled through the rest of the comedian's set, even after the attention wasn't on him.

The king was quiet on the way back to the castle. "I know you're upset, but he was seriously funny," the queen said.

"Good grief! I can't believe you thought he was funny," the king said. He turned away from her.

"Are you in ill health?" she asked, feeling his forehead. "You normally have a good sense of humor. But most of his jokes went over like a lead balloon with you."

"It's like you think he's the living end of comedians," the king retorted. "He's old news, a one-man band, a wise fool." The king gasped.

"What is it, dear?"

Chapter 11: Oxymorons

"I said that in a loud whisper with a sad smile. Do you know what that means?"

"No, but you look like the living dead."

"Oxymoron. His success in comedy is causing overuse of oxymorons. It will be a minor miracle if we can fix this. Ack! Now I'm using one of the comedian's oxymorons."

It was late when the couple returned to the castle, so the king didn't awaken the children. But the next morning at breakfast, he told them there was a problem.

The queen shared her perspective. "My unbiased opinion is that your father's feelings were hurt. The comedian said that the staff's code name for him is Jumbo Shrimp."

Cook's laughter could be heard from the kitchen.

"Okay. That's enough from the loyal opposition," the king said tersely. "The popularity of Oxymoron's comedy has people overusing oxymorons."

When the kids asked what oxymorons were, he was prepared. He opened *The Guide to Grammar Galaxy* to its article on them.

Oxymorons

Oxymorons are figures of speech that are a combination of literal opposites. The word oxymoron itself is contradictory meaning both "sharp" and "dull or foolish." Some examples of oxymorons are:

icy hot
small fortune
genuine imitation

Oxymorons are often used in sarcastic and political humor. In everyday use, recognition of the **incongruity** of the oxymoron may be lost. For example, we don't notice the opposite meanings in these word pairings:

crash landing
freezer burn
original copy

Chapter 11: Oxymorons

> **An oxymoron is not the same as a paradox.** Oxymorons are contradictory words or groups of words, while a paradox is a contradictory or nonsensical statement that has truth to it. For example, Shakespeare's Hamlet says, "I must be cruel to be kind." Hamlet planned to avenge his father's murder. But the statement can be interpreted to mean that we can do something painful for another's good.
>
> **Avoid using oxymorons in formal writing.** In humorous writing, choose oxymorons that retain their contradiction because they aren't in everyday use.

"If oxymorons are being overused, what should we do?" Ellen asked.

"Act naturally," Kirk answered.

Ellen frowned in response. "That makes no sense."

"I'm clearly confused, too," Luke added.

★ ★ ★ ★ ★ ★ ★ ★ ★ ★

incongruity – *oddness*
vogue – *fashion*

★ ★ ★ ★ ★ ★ ★ ★ ★ ★

"That's the problem with using too many oxymorons," the king said.

"Wait! I have an idea. Oxymoron is in **vogue**, right?" Ellen asked. The rest of the family nodded. "What if we have the guardians using so many oxymorons that everyone gets tired of them? They'll stop seeing the comedian. His popularity will grow smaller."

"I love it, Ellen," the queen said.

"The plan gets a definite maybe from me," Luke said.

The king agreed it was worth a try, though he wondered how he could bear even more oxymorons in the short-term.

The children got to work on a mission called Oxymorons, while the king planned to do an extra-long workout in the gym.

What does *incongruity* mean?

What is an oxymoron?

Why do you think the king wanted to work out longer than usual?

Chapter 12

The children were excited about their field trip to the science center. The group was gathered at the main station, waiting for their space tram.

Luke chattered with friends about their favorite exhibits and what they planned to do first. Luke was looking forward to the special exhibit on the future of gaming most. He would have the opportunity to try new technology before it was available to the public.

Ellen talked about the hairstyle exhibit with her friends. She couldn't wait to sit in the machine that would temporarily change the color and style of her hair. She was talking about her desire to try curly hair when the group's space tram became visible.

The children instinctively moved closer to the platform until they saw something was wrong. The tram wasn't slowing down. What was worse is the tram appeared to be off its path. It was heading right for them!

The field trip leader shouted for the students to get out of the way. The group bolted up the grassy hill to the left of the platform. They watched in horror and the tram passed them and slammed into the hillside. The steel of the lead car collapsed like an accordion, and the following cars lay littered on the tracks in a zig-zag pattern.

The children were quaking in shock at what they'd just witnessed. The field trip leader asked Kirk to call for emergency assistance. She ordered the students to stay where they were. She then rushed down the tracks to the cars, looking for victims.

She looked up to the tram windows, expecting to see passengers peering down at her. But there were none. Satisfied that there were no crash victims, the leader returned to her students to console them.

Soon, emergency personnel arrived on the scene. One police officer approached the field trip leader and students and said he had a few questions for them.

Chapter 12: Onomatopoeia

"Of course," the leader responded graciously.

"I imagine you're all a little **shaken** by this experience." Many in the group nodded and trembled. "Understandable. It will take some time, but talking about it will **soothe** you. Let's start with what you saw."

★ ★ ★ ★ ★ ★ ★ ★ ★ ★

shaken – *traumatized*
soothe – *calm*
numbly – *dazedly*

★ ★ ★ ★ ★ ★ ★ ★ ★ ★

"We saw the tram coming up that hill, and we thought everything was fine. But it wasn't slowing down. At first, I thought maybe it wasn't supposed to stop here. But then I saw that it was off its path and was heading right for us," the leader said, shuddering.

"Go on," the officer said, sympathizing.

"I yelled for the students to get out of the way. We ran up that grassy hill there. A few seconds later, the tram slammed into the hillside there. It just missed us," she said with tears threatening.

"Yes, it did. And we are thankful that you're all safe."

"Yes, I can't imagine otherwise," the leader said, dabbing at her eyes with a tissue.

"Just a few more questions. Did you hear brake sounds as the tram approached the stop?"

"No. Come to think of it, no, I did not. Did you children hear brake sounds?" she asked. The children **numbly** shook their heads that they had not.

"Okay. So the brakes weren't working. Did you hear any other sounds that might give us a clue as to what went wrong?"

"Hm. No. But it's all a blur now," the leader said apologetically.

"But you heard the impact of the tram, of course," the officer said.

The leader stared blankly at him. "No. As a matter of fact, there was no sound." She turned to the children for confirmation. "Did you hear the tram hit the hillside?"

A chorus of children reporting what they'd seen began with lots of gesturing.

"Yes, children, but did you hear anything?"

The students stopped to think and then slowly shook their heads. They hadn't heard anything at all.

"Curious," the officer said, taking notes. "All right. We have alerted the children's parents. They are on their way to pick them up. Go home and trust that we will determine what caused the accident."

Chapter 12: Onomatopoeia

The king and queen arrived shortly thereafter and embraced their children in relief.

"You poor dears!" the queen said tearfully. "You must have been terrified."

Ellen nodded and hugged her mother tightly. Kirk agreed that it was an unnerving experience.

"They don't know why the tram didn't make any sounds," Luke interjected.

"What are you talking about?" the king asked. "It had to have made sounds when it crashed."

"It didn't." Kirk and Ellen voiced their agreement with Luke.

"That's impossible!" the king said. When he saw the look on his children's faces, he decided to drop it. Most likely the shock kept them from hearing anything, he thought. He was eager to get them home where they would feel safe.

When the royal family walked in the door, Comet met them, tail wagging. He was opening his mouth to give them a vocal greeting, but they couldn't hear him.

"That's funny," Kirk said. "Comet has laryngitis."

The king frowned. "If Comet had laryngitis, we would hear something. Comet, speak, boy!" he urged. Comet was complying but they could not hear anything. "Something is wrong," the king said. "You children go have a snack. I know Cook will want to see you. I'm going to get to the bottom of this."

The king went to his office and asked Screen for a status report on planet Vocabulary. "Your Highness, the only news I have is that the Onomatopoeia Union is on strike. They say they are working two jobs when the rest of the words have just one."

"Of all the nonsense!" the king said. He sighed and stroked his beard. This was a crisis he would need his children's help to handle, even though they were still recovering.

He obtained *The Guide to Grammar Galaxy* from the library and went to find the children. They were in the kitchen, eating and reviewing the accident with Cook. "Oh, my stars!" Cook exclaimed. "I'm so thankful you're all okay," she said, hugging each of them.

"I'm afraid we have more problems than just this tram accident," the king said to them. "I trust the Transporation Authority to determine the malfunction with the tram. But there is another problem only you three can solve." The king encouraged the kids to finish their snack. He then invited them into the dining room, so he could share what was happening.

He explained about the Onomatopoeia Union strike and then read the article on onomatopoeia from the guidebook.

Onomatopoeia
Onomatopoeia is the naming of a thing or action that represents its sound. It is a descriptive literary device that appeals to the reader's sense of hearing. You can remember onomatopoeia as sound nouns, though some of the words can also be used as verbs. For example, *slap* is both a sound and the act of hitting with the palm. YourDictionary.com organizes onomatopoeia into five main types of sounds: 1. **Collision sounds** often begin with cl- or th- and may end with -ng. (clang, thud, screech) 2. **Animal sounds** often have the long vowel sounds /oo/ or /ay/. (moo, bray, buzz) 3. **Vocal sounds** often begin with gr- or mu-. (grunt, murmur, belch) 4. **Water sounds** often begin with dr- or sp-. (drip, splash, bloop) 5. **Air sounds** often start with wh- or end in -sh. (whoosh, swish, gasp)

"So, the strike kept us from hearing the tram crash?" Kirk asked.

"And kept us from hearing Comet bark?" Luke added.

"Yes, I'm afraid so," the king answered.

"Onomatopoeia words are essential. Can't you order them back to work?" Ellen asked, hopefully.

"I could, Ellen. But I prefer to encourage them instead. That's where you three come in. If you could explain to them that they aren't doing more jobs than other words, I think that would end the strike. Most onomatopoeia is just sounds. Some of them will be sent to work in Verb Village, but they won't be doing double duty."

"We have to talk to a lot of onomatopoeia words. We'll need the guardians' help for sure," Luke said.

"That's what I was thinking," the king said, smiling.

"As long as we don't have to get on a space tram, I'm okay with going to planet Vocabulary," Ellen said, shuddering.

"I understand why you would feel that way, Ellen. And until we determine the cause of the crash, I don't want you on a tram. But you will have to ride one again. Otherwise, your fear of trams will keep

Chapter 12: Onomatopoeia

growing. You might even become afraid of every form of transportation. We fight fear by facing it."

"Like the Gremlin!" Luke said, punching the air playfully.

The king laughed. "Yes, like that. You can use the space porter to travel after you send out an Onomatopoeia mission."

The children got to work and the king contacted the Transportation Authority.

What does *soothe* mean?

What is one type of onomatopoeia sound?

Why didn't the students hear the tram accident?

Chapter 13

"Luke, how are you liking the new game Happy Holographics sent you?" the king asked one Saturday morning.

Luke was in the middle of playing it when his father came into the media room. "It's amazing!" Luke exclaimed. "Watch this," he said, as he climbed onto an eagle's back to soar above an advancing army of bears.

"I'm sure it is amazing," the king said. "But I can't see anything," he said, laughing.

"Oh, yeah," Luke said, laughing and removing his virtual reality headset. "Wanna try?" he asked his father.

"Maybe later," the king said, smiling. "When are you going to start your review? You promised the company you would provide them with a written review—and not just a thank-you note," the king reminded his son.

"Maybe later?" Luke joked. "I'll start it this afternoon. I want to play some more so I know what the levels are like."

"That sounds like a good plan. Have fun," the king said before leaving the room.

When Luke began working on his review later that day, he was surprised that it didn't seem like work. He loved the new game he'd received, and he wanted all of his friends to know about it. He wrote a first draft that he was happy with. Then he went to take Comet for a walk.

Over the next few days, Luke added more descriptive language to his review. He varied the beginnings of his sentences. He read it aloud and looked for errors. He used a spell checker, too. He felt it was ready for his mother to review before he sent it to Happy Holographics.

The queen smiled and nodded as she read through his review. "Luke, I'm impressed! Your writing has improved so much. And I can tell that you checked the paper for errors thoroughly. I only found one homonym error. You used the word threw (t-h-r-e-w) for through (t-h-r-o-u-g-h). The shorter *threw* means to toss something and you wanted the *through* that means traveling or moving."

Luke nodded, pleased with his mother's praise for his work.

"The only other recommendation I have is to change the title. It's not very compelling," the queen said.

"Oh, right. I forgot to brainstorm different title ideas. I'll do that now," Luke said. He wrote several ideas down and asked his mother which she liked best. Then he contacted Kirk via communicator and asked him for his favorite of their top three. After Kirk chose one, the queen encouraged Luke to make the changes and get the review sent off. "Make sure you include a thank-you for the game in your communication with the company," she said.

"I will, Mother," Luke said, smiling. He left with his paper, eager to have the task completed.

A week later, the king and queen asked Luke if he'd heard anything from Happy Holographics about his review. Luke scowled.

"What is it?" the queen asked with concern. "Didn't they like your review? I thought you did so well on it."

"I thought so, too," Luke said. "But I still can't spell. They sent it back to me with my spelling errors changed. I shouldn't write reviews for any company. It's so embarrassing," Luke said, **shamefaced**.

★ ★ ★ ★ ★ ★ ★ ★ ★

shamefaced – *embarrassed*
recanted – *took it back*

★ ★ ★ ★ ★ ★ ★ ★ ★

"Did you change the review after I looked at it? The only spelling error I saw was the homophone," the queen said.

"I changed that and the title. That's it," Luke said with an irritated tone.

"Dear, did you miss spelling errors in Luke's review? I'm surprised at you when his reputation and confidence were at stake," the king said, frowning.

The queen's eye's blazed. "I did not miss spelling errors," she said tersely.

"Were you tired? Distracted? Maybe you need reading glasses. You're not getting any younger, you know," the king said. When he saw his wife's expression, he **recanted**. "Or perhaps the company's editor can't spell," he said sheepishly.

"Could I see what the company sent you?" the queen asked.

Luke pulled up the file on his communicator and displayed it on the screen in front of them. The king and queen scanned the review and noted the changes marked. They looked at one another and smiled. Then they laughed.

"I'm sorry I questioned your spelling, dear," the king said. "I should have known better."

"Yes, you should have," the queen agreed teasingly. "And you're not getting any younger, either. You'll need reading glasses before I do."

"Most likely," the king said, smiling.

"I don't get it. Why are you two happy about my spelling errors all of a sudden?" Luke asked.

"Luke, you did not have any spelling errors," the king said.

"What? Then why have they changed these words? Is the Gremlin working at Happy Holographics?"

Chapter 13: British Spelling

The king laughed. "Not that I know of. The spelling changes they've made are British spellings," he explained.

"British spellings? I don't understand," Luke said.

"I think it's time we explained it to you and your siblings," the king said. He had Kirk and Ellen brought to the sunroom along with *The Guide to Grammar Galaxy*.

When they arrived, the king read the entry on British vs. American English spelling.

British vs. American English Spelling
English spelling was inconsistent until the publication of two dictionaries—Johnson's *A Dictionary of the English Language* in 1755 and Webster's *An American Dictionary of the English Language* in 1828. British English uses more French-dialect spellings of English words. These spelling preferences were generally adopted by former territories of the British Empire. Spelling changes in America and the United Kingdom developed independently. Canadian spelling incorporates both British and American rules. Australia uses less American spelling than Canada but more than New Zealand, which uses British spelling almost exclusively. **-our/-or** Unstressed ending syllables are spelled -our in British English and -or in American English. **-re/-er** British words ending in -bre or -tre are spelled -ber or -ter in American English. **-ise/-ize** British English mostly uses -ise at the end of words while American English uses -ize. **-ll/-l** British and American English use a double ll for different words. **-e** British English often keeps a silent -e when adding a suffix, whereas American English does not. A table of some common words spelled differently in British and American English follows.

Chapter 13: British Spelling

British vs. American Spelling of Common Words			
British	American	British	American
colour	color	neighbour	neighbor
centre	center	theatre	theater
organise	organize	realise	realize
cancelled	canceled	traveller	traveler
enrol	enroll	enthral	enthrall
ageing	aging	likeable	likable

"So, my spelling wasn't wrong? I was just using American English spelling?" Luke asked with a hopeful tone.

"That's right, Luke," the king answered with a grin.

"Do I have to change my spelling then?" Luke continued.

"Yes, we should use the spelling preferred by a website or publication," the king said.

Luke **quashed** a groan.

✶ ✶ ✶ ✶ ✶ ✶ ✶ ✶ ✶ ✶

quashed – *suppressed*

✶ ✶ ✶ ✶ ✶ ✶ ✶ ✶ ✶ ✶

"Do a lot of people use British spelling, rather than English spelling?" Kirk asked.

"As a matter of fact, yes," the king replied.

"I'm wondering if this would make a good mission for the guardians then," Kirk said.

"Splendid idea, son," the king answered.

The three English children got to work on a mission called British vs. American English spelling.

What does *shamefaced* mean?

What is one spelling difference between British and American English?

Why did Happy Holographics correct Luke's spelling?

70

Chapter 14

"Look what came in the mail for me!" Luke declared. He waved it in the air as he addressed his parents.

"I hope it's not a bill," the king quipped.

"No, it's an invitation," Luke said, beaming.

"To a birthday party?" the queen asked.

"Better!" Luke said. "I've been invited to tour the headquarters of Happy Holographics!"

The queen clapped in appreciation and stood to hug her son. "I'm excited for you! When do they want you?"

"Two weeks."

"It's smart publicity for them," the king said.

"I'm sure it is, but I think they know how amazing our boy is," the queen said, ruffling Luke's hair.

Luke beamed again. "I'm going to tell Kirk," he said, leaving the room with a bounce in his step.

The visit couldn't come soon enough for Luke. The company had assured the king and queen that Luke would be in good hands. Their presence wouldn't be **requisite**.

★ ★ ★ ★ ★ ★ ★ ★ ★ ★

requisite – *necessary*

★ ★ ★ ★ ★ ★ ★ ★ ★ ★

The queen had made sure Luke had packed everything he might need for the trip. She reminded him to use his best manners. Luke promised that he would and that he would talk to them via communicator.

He hugged his family and his dog Comet goodbye and boarded a space tram heading to Manchester. The king didn't wait for his wife's tears. "He'll be fine," he said reassuringly.

The queen nodded her agreement quietly. "It's going to be quiet without him," Ellen noted.

The rest of the family somberly agreed.

Chapter 14: British Vocabulary

"But it will be exciting to hear about his visit," Kirk said, attempting to lighten the mood.

The king wanted to continue the positive **sentiment**. "I have an idea. Let's get some ice cream!"

The queen hugged her husband. "You know how to cheer me up," she said, smiling.

★ ★ ★ ★ ★ ★ ★ ★ ★

sentiment – *feeling*

sublime – *magnificent*

★ ★ ★ ★ ★ ★ ★ ★ ★

Upon arrival, Luke was greeted by a man in a top hat. "You must be Master Luke. I'm with Happy Holographics. I'll be escorting you to your lodging and then to the company," he said warmly.

"That will be **sublime**," Luke answered.

The man smiled at his word choice and took Luke's luggage. He led him to a vehicle and asked Luke to get into the back seat. "I'll just put your luggage in the boot."

The boot? Luke thought to himself. *How can you put luggage in a boot?* He saw that the man had opened the trunk of the car. *He must have a boot in there*, Luke thought.

"Are you on holiday?" the driver asked Luke as he got behind the wheel of the vehicle.

Luke frowned. *Was it one of those minor holidays he had forgotten about?* "I'm sorry. I don't know what holiday it is," he said.

The man smiled in the rearview mirror at the strange boy. "I like your jumper," he said. "Very sharp."

Luke's eyes grew wide. *What jumper?* He looked down and noticed that he was nervously twitching his leg. He tried to stop.

The driver was exasperated with traffic and mumbled his complaint. "I can't see around this lorry."

Who's Lorry? Luke wondered.

"Say, Luke. I've been fighting some kind of bug. Would you mind if I stopped at the chemist's shop on the way?"

"Uh, sure. That's fine," Luke stammered.

The driver pulled up to a building, stopped the vehicle, and asked Luke to wait for him.

The driver emerged from the building, carrying a bag. He told Luke, "I had to get some nappies and a new dummy for the wife, too," he said apologetically.

Chapter 14: British Vocabulary

He got a dummy in the store? I'm not supposed to use that word. And what's this about taking naps for his wife? What a strange man, Luke thought.

Luke was impressed by the entrance to Happy Holographics' headquarters as their vehicle stopped in front of it. A holograph of two players engaged in battle captivated Luke. He and his escort walked through it.

A woman with a friendly face greeted him inside the building. She said she would be his hostess for the day. She led him to a meeting room. "I'm sorry about this, but we have to begin by having you meet with our barrister. Would you like a biscuit while you wait?"

Luke was confused, so he said, "No, thank you" with a smile. *What's a barrister?* he wondered.

A man soon entered the room and shook Luke's hand. "I have some simple paperwork for you to sign. It just says that you agree not to share any information about our projects. They're top secret. Understand?" Luke nodded. "Okay. Sign your name next to the X."

Luke did as he was told, glad that his mother had regularly made him practice his signature. The man thanked him and left the room with the papers. The hostess told him they were ready to start the tour.

Luke had a wonderful time meeting the game designers. They were happy to explain how they went about creating new games from start to finish.

Later, the hostess asked if he was ready for lunch. He said he was. His nervousness had made him hungry. "We have a sandwich for you. Would you like some crisps, too?" she asked.

Luke thought for a moment. He had no idea what crisps were. If he said he wanted them and they weren't good, he would have to eat them to have good manners. "No, thank you," he said graciously.

"I could get you some chips if you prefer," she said.

"Yes! I love chips," Luke said gratefully.

When lunch arrived, Luke was surprised that the hostess had potato chips with her sandwich and he had French fries. *She must have forgotten that I said chips*, he thought.

After lunch, Luke was allowed to test some new games. He was led to a darkened room. The hostess said, "You'll need a torch to go in." While Luke was wondering why they would use torches inside a building, the woman produced a flashlight and handed it to him. *She must have realized a torch was a bad idea,* he thought.

Luke loved the games he tested and was complimentary of the design team. The team beamed with pride at Luke's enthusiasm. One programmer said, "We don't get to interact with gamers much. It's been wonderful meeting you, Luke."

The hostess told Luke his driver had been called. "Why don't we play naughts and crosses while we wait?" she said.

"Cool! They didn't show me that game," Luke said.

"You haven't played naughts and crosses?" she asked in surprise.

"No. Do we have to go back into the game room?" he asked.

The woman smiled. "No. But let's go back and play your favorite game from today instead. I'll have the driver contact me when he's here."

When Luke got into the vehicle later, his driver was agitated that he was late. "First I got stuck behind the dustman and then a juggernaut."

"What game is that? I don't think I've played that one yet," Luke said.

The driver studied Luke in the rearview mirror. "You're an interesting fellow, Luke English. But I like you!" He smiled and returned Luke to his lodging. A chaperone would be staying in a room next to his, he explained.

"Have safe travels home," the driver said. Luke thanked him and went immediately to his room. He couldn't wait to talk with his family.

He contacted his father via his communicator and waited while the king gathered the rest of the family.

"So how was it?" the king asked.

"Good! I got to test some new games and they're amazing!" Luke gushed.

"What are they like?" Kirk asked.

"I can't say," Luke answered. "I had some guy they call a barrister make me swear not to tell."

"It's understandable that they don't want you to share company secrets," the king said.

"Did they treat you well? What did they feed you?" the queen asked.

Chapter 14: British Vocabulary

"Oh, yes," Luke replied. "But they seemed confused about my food request. I asked for chips and they served me French fries. But that was after they asked me if I wanted crisps. So weird.

"There were other strange things they said, but I can't tell you. I promised not to discuss my visit with anyone."

The king and queen smiled at one another. "Luke, you must respect their wishes not to discuss the company's new games. But you can tell us other things they said. I have a feeling you encountered British vocabulary," the king said.

When Luke asked what he meant, the king asked for *The Guide to Grammar Galaxy*. He read the article on British Vocabulary to the family.

British Vocabulary

Although English speakers can understand both American and British English, there are some notable differences in vocabulary. These differences developed as English speakers moved to other countries and established unique dialects. However, advances in global communication have diminished the vocabulary differences. Some remaining differences between American and British English are listed in the chart below.

American	British
attorney	barrister, solicitor
cookie	biscuit
trunk	boot
drug store	chemist's
french fries	chips
stove	cooker
crib	cot
pacifier	dummy
jumper	sweater
garbage collector	dustman
generator	dynamo
overpass	flyover
billboard	hoarding
vacation	holiday
elevator	lift

Chapter 14: British Vocabulary

American	British
truck	lorry
diaper	nappy
nursing home	private hospital
sidewalk	pavement
gasoline	petrol
mailbox	postbox
potato chips	crisps
stroller	push-chair
line	queue
can	tin
flashlight	torch

"That explains a lot!" Luke exclaimed. "Like why my driver put my luggage in the boot."

Kirk and Ellen laughed.

"I started to wonder if something was wrong with me," Luke added.

"Father, I bet this isn't the first time someone has been confused by British vs. American English. Perhaps we should create a mission on the subject?" Kirk suggested.

"Brilliant idea! Luke, I should have prepared you for the vocabulary differences before your visit," the king apologized.

"No problem, Father. It made the visit even more interesting," Luke said.

Kirk and Ellen promised to work on a British Vocabulary mission while Luke enjoyed his night away from home.

"I'm going to order crisps from room service," he joked.

What does *requisite* mean?

What is the barrister's job?

Why are there differences in American and British vocabulary?

Chapter 15

"What is it, dear?" the king asked his wife. She was sitting in the media room, frowning.

"I just looked over the messages Ellen has been sending with her communicator," the queen answered.

"And? Has she been talking to boys?" The king looked worried, too.

"No," the queen said, laughing. "It's not that serious."

"What then?"

"It's just that she is using the wrong vocabulary words."

The king laughed. "Is that all? She's a child and children make vocabulary errors."

The queen sighed. "I know. It's just that—"

"What?"

"I'm afraid that her vocabulary is declining because of text messaging her friends," the queen said gravely.

"Hm. Do you think she could be trying not to appear too smart?"

"It's possible. What do you think we should do?" the queen asked.

"Are you thinking we should take her communicator away?"

"Vocabulary is so important. It might be worth her being upset with us for now," the queen said.

"You may be right. If you think it's best, I'll support you," the king said, patting his wife on the shoulder.

"All right. I'll tell her tomorrow," the queen said sadly.

The announcement that Ellen's communicator would be taken away was not well received. "What do you mean my vocabulary isn't good? I'm talking to my friends. I'm not writing a formal paper," she complained.

"I know, dear. But if you keep writing this way, you won't know proper vocabulary when you are writing a formal paper," the queen said **judiciously**.

✶ ✶ ✶ ✶ ✶ ✶ ✶ ✶ ✶

judiciously – *carefully*

impertinent – *disrespectful*

✶ ✶ ✶ ✶ ✶ ✶ ✶ ✶ ✶

Ellen's lips trembled and her eyes filled with tears. "It's not fair! You're going to take away my communicator but not the boys'? Do they always use good vocabulary? I doubt it!" Ellen's hands were clenched into fists and she was yelling.

"I understand that you're upset, but that's no excuse for being **impertinent** with your mother," the king said sternly.

"Ugh! I can't believe this!" Ellen yelled as she stormed out of the room.

The king went to follow her, but the queen encouraged him to let her go and calm down.

"I'm glad I don't message my friends as much as Ellen. And I'm doubly glad I don't have girl emotions!" Luke joked.

The king chuckled, but the queen gave him a chastising glance.

Chapter 15: Confused Vocabulary

The next day at breakfast, Ellen seemed calmer. "I'm sorry you were upset, Ellen. I expect that you'll get your communicator back soon. I'd like you to do some writing to practice correct vocabulary," the queen said.

"Just me?" Ellen asked, her voice rising.

The queen responded quickly to prevent tears. "No, of course not. The boys will be writing as well."

Luke groaned and Kirk sighed.

"I shouldn't have to remind you, boys, how important proper vocabulary is," the king said firmly.

The two boys nodded and ate their breakfast.

Later that day, the queen was reviewing the children's responses to a writing prompt. The queen gasped while reading Luke's paper. "Luke, you used the word supposably."

"Yes, supposably we will one day be able to grow new body parts."

"Eww," Ellen said, wrinkling her nose. "Disgusting."

"It's not disgusting if you lose your leg," Luke retorted.

"That's not what I'm reacting to. *Supposably* means something is capable of being imagined," the queen said.

"Right. I am capable of imagining a day when we could grow new body parts," Luke replied.

"That's not what you said," the queen responded.

"Supposably that's not what I said," Luke answered.

The queen was getting exasperated. "Luke, you misused several vocabulary words in your writing."

"Does he get his communicator taken away?" Ellen asked hopefully.

"Hey!" Luke complained, glaring at his sister.

"Maybe not his communicator, but I'm wondering if your game time is ruining your vocabulary," the queen told Luke.

"It isn't! My vocabulary is great!" Luke objected.

The queen ignored him and began reading Kirk's writing. "Kirk, you spelled principal with an *a*, when it's clear you mean the other principle," she said.

"What?" Kirk said with some annoyance.

The queen repeated herself. "What difference does it make?" Kirk asked. He regretted his response when he saw his mother's expression.

"You three need to go to your bedchambers and think about your attitudes. And I'll take your communicators, Kirk and Luke."

The boys were shocked but handed over their devices. Ellen suppressed a smile. She was glad she wasn't the only one banned from her communicator.

That evening, the queen was complaining about the children's attitudes to the king. "And their vocabulary keeps getting worse!" she said.

"Ah, dear, don't worry. I want to insure you that their vocabulary and their attitudes will improve," the king said.

"What did you say?" the queen asked, eyes wide.

"I said I want to insure you that everything will be okay."

"That's what I thought."

"You don't have to complement me. I know I'm a great husband," he teased.

"Uh, right. I know," the queen said haltingly. "Thank you."

"I'm going to do some historic reading before bed. I'm determined to have less books in my to-read pile. Do you want me to read in my office? I won't keep you up that way," the king said.

"Uh, yes. That's very gracious of you," the queen said.

As soon as the king closed the door, the queen asked Screen via her tablet for a status report on planet Vocabulary.

"The masquerade ball is going on as we speak, Your Highness," Screen reported.

"A masquerade ball? You mean words are in costume?"

"I believe so," Screen replied.

"Hm. I'm sure that's the problem. Is it over tonight?"

"No, the organizer says it won't end until every word is in costume."

"Oh, dear," the queen said worriedly. "I'm going to have to interrupt the king's historic reading."

The king was surprised when the queen knocked on his office door. She explained that the masquerade ball was causing vocabulary confusion. As it was late, the two decided to wait until morning to tell the children.

The next morning at breakfast, the queen explained what was happening to vocabulary as a result of the ball.

Chapter 15: Confused Vocabulary

"You mean I can have my communicator back?" Ellen said with relief.

"Us too?" Luke asked.

"Yes," the queen said smiling. "I'm sorry I assumed the confusion was your fault. But even when we are wrong, we expect you to respect us," the queen said.

The children nodded solemnly.

"We are going to need you three to go to planet Vocabulary to get this mess sorted out. You'll need this information from the guidebook," the king said. He read the article called "Commonly Confused Vocabulary" aloud.

✯ ✯ ✯ ✯ ✯ ✯ ✯ ✯ ✯ ✯

differentiated – *separated*

✯ ✯ ✯ ✯ ✯ ✯ ✯ ✯ ✯ ✯

Commonly Confused Vocabulary
Some commonly confused vocabulary words can be **differentiated** by their part of speech, unique spelling, or specific meaning. Consult the chart below for words that are commonly misused. The highlighted words are homophones that are pronounced similarly, leading to confusion.

Commonly Confused Vocabulary Words					
Word	Part of Speech; Meaning	Word	Part of Speech; Meaning	Word	Part of Speech; Meaning
a lot	Article, Noun; many	alot	misspelling	allot	Verb; give as share; set apart
awhile	Adv.; done a short time	a while	Noun; period of time		
among	Prep.; amid 3 or more items not specified	between	Prep.; in the middle of 2 or more specific items		
assure	Verb; tell to remove doubt	ensure	Verb; make certain	insure	Verb; provide security for
capital	Noun; city seat of government	capitol	Noun; legislative building		

Chapter 15: Confused Vocabulary

Word	Part of Speech; Meaning	Word	Part of Speech; Meaning	Word	Part of Speech; Meaning
complement	**Noun**; thing that completes **Verb**; make perfect	compliment	**Noun**; expression of praise **Verb**; commend		
emigrate	**Verb**; leave country to live elsewhere	immigrate	**Verb**; come to country to live		
historic	**Adj.**; important in history	historical	**Adj.**; about the past		
i.e.	**Abbrev.**; in other words	e.g.	**Abbrev.**; for example		
into	**Prep.**; indicates where	in to	**Adv., Prep.**; indicates purpose		
less	**Adj.**; used with uncountable nouns	fewer	**Adj.**; used with countable nouns		
login	**Noun**; process to gain computer access	log in	**Verb, Prep.**; start a computer or system session		
principal	**Noun**; school director	principle	**Noun**; value		
stationary	**Adj.**; immovable	stationery	**Noun**; printed paper		
supposably	**Adv.**; may be conceived or imagined	supposedly	**Adv.**; truth is doubtful		

Abbrev.= abbreviation; Adj.= adjective; Adv.= adverb; Prep.=preposition

"This reminds me of when we learned about tricky homophones," Kirk said.

"Yes, we learned that we could tell some homophones apart by part of speech," Ellen said.

"Determining which vocabulary word is which at the masquerade ball seems like a lot of work, and I mean a-space-l-o-t," Luke said.

"That's right, Luke. You will need to send a mission to the guardians so they can help you. I will make sure that Grammar Patrol is there to keep new words from entering the ball," the king said.

The children sent out a mission called Confused Vocabulary Words. Then they gratefully collected their communicators and left for planet Vocabulary.

Chapter 15: Confused Vocabulary

What does *impertinent* mean?

What word should Luke have used instead of *supposably*?

What event was happening on planet Vocabulary that caused wrong words to be used?

Chapter 16

Luke was helping Cook clean in the kitchen. He wasn't fond of doing chores, but he was very fond of talking with Cook.

"Luke, will you take this trash out for the garbage man?" Cook asked.

"Sure will," Luke answered cheerfully.

"Now what is it they call the garbage man in Manchester?" she asked.

"Oh, yes. It's—hm. I can't remember," Luke admitted.

"I can hardly chastise you for not remembering when I don't remember myself!" she said, laughing.

"Right," Luke said, smiling. "I have it written in my Word Book. I'll tell you later."

"Wonderful. Oh, wait. Will you add this can to the trash? What do they call a can in Manchester? You told me they have a different word for it."

"Right. They call it a, a. Hm. I can't remember that, either," Luke admitted.

"Was it a tin?" Cook asked.

"Yes! That's it," Luke replied.

"I think their funniest word is the word for pacifier."

"Yes! So funny!" Luke agreed.

"You remember what it is, right?" Cook asked.

"Of course!" Luke said.

"So, what is it?" Cook asked, her eyes narrowing a bit.

"*You* know what it is," Luke said, warmth beginning to creep up his neck.

"Yes, I do. But do you?"

Luke hung his head. "No," he said in a whisper.

"Dummy."

Luke's jaw dropped and his eyes widened. He grabbed the bag of trash and **scurried** out the door with it. When he returned to the kitchen, Cook asked if anything was wrong. He didn't respond, leaving the kitchen without a word.

★ ★ ★ ★ ★ ★ ★ ★ ★ ★

scurried – *hurried*
quandary – *dilemma*
composed – *unemotional*

★ ★ ★ ★ ★ ★ ★ ★ ★ ★

Cook scratched her head, wondering what had gotten into young Luke. She decided he had forgotten something important and would be back.

Luke found his mother in her study. She appeared to be deep in thought, but he had a **quandary** important enough to interrupt her. He waited patiently for his mother to notice his presence.

"Luke!" she said warmly. "Are you finished helping Cook in the kitchen?"

Despite his intention to be **composed**, he couldn't hold back the tears.

"Luke, what's wrong?" she asked, astonished by his upset.

"It's Cook. Well, maybe it's me," he said in a rush, choking back sobs.

"Oh, dear. Tell me what happened."

"Well, she asked me what the British call a garbage man. And I couldn't remember. Then she asked me what they call a can. She said it was a tin. I knew it! But I couldn't remember. Then she asked me what they call a pacifier and when I couldn't remember, she called me a dummy," Luke said, sniffling.

The queen covered her mouth to hide a grin but not before Luke noticed.

"You think I'm a dummy, too?" Luke asked, horrified at the thought.

"Luke, no!" the queen exclaimed. "Don't you remember that the British word for pacifier is *dummy*?"

Luke was going to defend himself when he realized what his mother had said. "The driver said he got his wife a dummy. It's the word for pacifier. Ugh. I really feel like a dummy now!"

"Luke, sometimes we misunderstand people because we hear what we want to hear. Or in your case, we hear what we're afraid to hear."

"What do you mean?"

Chapter 16: Vocabulary Mnemonics

"I mean that you were feeling foolish that you couldn't remember your British vocabulary words. When Cook said the word *dummy*, you assumed she was calling you a name."

"Are you saying *I* thought I was being a dummy?" Luke asked.

"Yes, but you aren't," the queen said, rubbing his shoulder.

"But why can't I remember these words?" he asked, pounding his fist into his palm in frustration.

"I think I can help," the queen said, smiling. "There are tricks called mnemonics that can help us remember vocabulary. They are just what you need. Let's ask Kirk and Ellen to join us in the library. I believe I've neglected to teach them about vocabulary mnemonics, too."

Once the queen and her children were seated in the castle library, she read them an entry from *The Guide to Grammar Galaxy*.

Vocabulary Mnemonics

Mnemonics are memory aids. They can be particularly helpful in learning vocabulary in English and other languages. Some memory helps to try include:

Create sayings that include parts of the word and its meaning. For example, the word *ubiquitous* means something is everywhere. Saying "The letter *u* is everywhere in the word ubiquitous" can help you remember its meaning. *Caveat* means a warning. Use the words *cave* and *eat* within the word to create the saying "*This cave will eat you* is a crazy warning."

Create a word picture using a word part or sound. Look for part of the word that you can use to create a memorable mental image of the word's meaning. For example, the word *paramount* means supreme or superior. *Para* also begins the words *paratrooper* and *parachuting*. *Mount* reminds us of a mountain. Imagine a paratrooper parachuting to a mountain and then enjoying a supreme pizza. The word *sanguine,* which means cheerful, sounds like penguin. Create a mental image of sanguine penguins on a water slide at the zoo. You can also create a cartoon to help you remember your word picture.

Listen to songs. Use a teacher-approved website to search for song lyrics that include the vocabulary word you want to memorize. Listening to and singing the song will help you remember the meaning of the word. For example, remember that *strife* means trouble by listening to and singing "The Bare Necessities" from *The Jungle Book* movie.

Chapter 16: Vocabulary Mnemonics

> **Use premade mnemonics.** If you are struggling to create a vocabulary mnemonic, use books or websites that include vocabulary cartoons. You can also consult an online mnemonic dictionary.

"One of the words I couldn't remember is what a garbage man is called in British English. What mnemonic would I use for that?" Luke asked.

"Oh, I remember!" Ellen exclaimed. "They call him a dustman."

"Luke, you know we sweep with a dustpan. Imagine a garbage man not only picking up our trash but sweeping up afterward with a dustpan. You could even use a saying like 'The dustman uses a dustpan,'" the queen said.

"That would be strange for him to sweep up like that," Luke said, chuckling.

"Yes, it would. The more unique and funny the image you use, the more likely you are to remember it," the queen said.

"The dustman uses a dustpan," Luke repeated to himself.

"I think these mnemonics could help all the guardians remember vocabulary words. Let's create a mission!" Ellen suggested.

Her brothers and mother agreed it was a good idea. But Luke asked Kirk and Ellen to work on a vocabulary mnemonics mission without him. He wanted to apologize to Cook for his behavior.

What is a quandary?

What is one way to remember the meaning of a vocabulary word?

Why did Luke assume Cook was calling him a dummy?

Chapter 17

The children were discussing the new Action Theme Park on planet Vocabulary when their father joined them in the media room.

"It sounds so cool!" Luke said.

"It does," Kirk said.

"And it's not as expensive as some theme parks," Ellen said for her father's benefit. "Could we go?" she asked sweetly.

The king sighed. "I'm not that excited about theme parks. They all seem the same to me."

"That's because you're not a kid. They *all* seem exciting to me," Luke joked.

"I'm sure that's true," the king said, smiling. "If you can talk your mother into taking you, I'll pay for it. How about that?"

The children cheered. They should have no problem getting her to agree.

When the time came for the queen to take them to the theme park, the king kissed his wife on the cheek. He wished her a good time.

"How do I always end up taking the kids to these kinds of things?" she challenged him playfully.

"Because you're the nice parent," the king joked back.

Kirk, Luke, and Ellen agreed and thanked her **profusely** for taking them.

★ ★ ★ ★ ★ ★ ★ ★ ★ ★

profusely – *abundantly*

★ ★ ★ ★ ★ ★ ★ ★ ★ ★

"You can thank me by keeping your rooms clean," she said, tousling Luke's hair.

"Sure thing!" Luke said. "Now let's go!"

The family laughed.

The four of them took the shuttle to planet Vocabulary and then a tram to the park. There were hundreds of people lined up outside the entrance. The queen groaned but soon relaxed when she saw how quickly the line was moving.

Once inside the park, they were amused by unicyclists who called out directions to the main attractions. Luke wanted to ride the Supersonic roller coaster. The queen hoped to avoid riding it with him. She was interested in the Micro Body ride. You entered a car that took you on a blood cell's journey through the human body. She just hoped it wouldn't make her nauseous.

Ellen wanted to ride the Thermo Wheel—a ferris wheel that looked like it was on fire. Kirk joked that they should ride the Hydro Plunge afterward.

To get to those rides, they were directed to take the Chrono Transport. The four of them agreed it was a fast, exhilarating ride itself.

They exited near a game booth called Inter Balloon Darts. Ellen was entranced by the stuffed unicorns that were prizes for winners. "How do you win?" she asked the man behind the counter.

"Unlike most dart games that are too hard to win, we ask you to land the dart between the balloons. You win a prize if you don't break a balloon with three darts."

"Wow!" Ellen exclaimed.

"How much is it?" the queen interjected. Her eyes widened in surprise at the **steep** price.

Ellen saw her mother's reaction and began pleading. "Look how cute these unicorns are. And I'll win one for sure!"

steep – *expensive*
cynically – *skeptically*

The queen bargained with Ellen to pay for part of it with birthday money. Ellen was jubilant when she was given three darts to throw.

"We have our first contestant of the day! Gather round to see how easy it is to win one of these cute unicorns!" the booth attendant called.

Ellen's first dart landed between the balloons on the board, and the English family members celebrated. When the second dart also landed between balloons, they applauded. By this time, a small group of spectators had gathered to cheer her on. The third dart, however, popped a balloon. Ellen couldn't believe it. The people watching expressed their sympathy.

Ellen hoped she could talk her mother into buying three more darts, but the queen refused.

Luke agreed. "Those things are always a ripoff," Luke said **cynically**.

As the group made their way to the Thermo Wheel ride, Luke made another observation. "They have a lot of word parts working here."

"I noticed that, too," Kirk said. "Prefixes, suffixes, and root words."

"It's nice when something like this provides jobs for the locals," the queen said.

"But don't they already have jobs?" Luke asked.

"Well, yes," the queen said after thinking a moment.

Just then a siren blared so loudly that the English family and everyone around them had to cover their ears. When it ended, an announcement was made. "Attention. We must evacuate the theme park immediately. We hope you've had an adventurous time. But now we ask you to exit the park courteously. Please make your way to the Chrono Transport."

Chapter 17: Prefixes, Suffixes & Root Words

The queen stopped an employee who was scribbling something on a clipboard. "Sir, can you tell me what the emergency is?" She asked.

"No," he answered curtly.

"No?" the queen parroted in disbelief. She walked over to another employee who was using a microphone to talk about the benefits of annual membership to the park. "Excuse me," the queen said when she stopped speaking. "Do you know why we are being asked to leave the park?"

"We ask people to leave the park every day," the woman said with a shrug.

Before she could begin using the microphone again, the queen said, "You don't mean that you ask people to leave early like this every day."

"Yes. That's what I mean," the woman said, dismissing her to use the microphone.

The queen turned away from her and addressed the children. "Something isn't right here. Stay put. We aren't leaving until I talk with your father." She used her communicator to contact her husband. When he answered, she explained that the park was evacuating them after just a short time.

"And they aren't giving you an explanation?" he asked.

"No. It seems that they do this daily."

"There's no electrical out—?" Did they apolog—?

"Dear, you're cutting out," the queen said.

"How myster—!" the king shouted. "Wait. I'm not cutting out. I'm not able to finish some of my words."

"You're not able to finish your words?"

Kirk whispered that he would like to talk to his father. When the queen handed him the communicator, he explained what he had noticed about the prefixes, suffixes, and root words working there.

"Good grammar! We can't have them working there. We won't be able to use them on planet English," the king exclaimed. "No doubt the Gremlin is behind this."

"What's worse is I don't think this is a real theme park. It's a scam," Kirk said quietly.

"I'll be dealing with their dishones—. Apparently, that suffix is working there, too. This is what we're going to do. Send me a list of all the prefixes, suffixes, and root words you see working at the park. Then I'll send out an emergency mission to the guardians," the king said.

"*You're* sending out a mission?" Kirk asked in surprise.

"Does that make you nerv—? Oh, for galaxy's sake, I was trying to make a joke. Yes, I'm sending out a mission on prefixes, suffixes, and root words. I'll be waiting on the list from you," the king said, ending the call.

Kirk told the rest of the family what the king had said. The four of them knew they had to work quickly to spot the word workers before they were forced to leave.

What does *profusely* mean?

Why was the king unable to finish some words?

What suffix is missing in the king's question, 'Does that make you nerv—'?

Chapter 18

"Luke, let's play laser tag in the garden tonight. I'm going to invite Max. You should invite Jimmy," Kirk said.

"Great idea!" Luke replied. "I'll contact him now." Luke used his communicator to call but got no answer. "I'll try again later," he told Kirk.

At lunch, the boys chatted enthusiastically about their laser tag game that evening.

"Who's joining you?" the queen asked.

"Max is coming and Luke invited Jimmy," Kirk replied.

"Well, I haven't actually talked to Jimmy. I'll call him again," Luke said, excusing himself. When he returned, his expression said that he hadn't been able to reach him.

"Maybe you should invite another friend so we know we have four," Kirk suggested.

"Maybe. I'll call again soon," Luke said, eating the rest of his sandwich.

"You could send him a text message. Kids don't always answer their communicators," Ellen said **astutely**.

"It's rude to ignore calls," the queen said.

Ellen shrugged and Luke said he would text Jimmy after lunch.

★ ★ ★ ★ ★ ★ ★ ★ ★ ★
astutely – *wisely*
shrill – *high-pitched*
★ ★ ★ ★ ★ ★ ★ ★ ★ ★

At dinner, Kirk asked Luke if Jimmy was all set to come over. Luke hesitated. "He didn't respond to your text?" Kirk asked with rising indignation.

"No—," Luke began before being interrupted by Kirk.

"Luke, we can't wait on him! Did you invite anyone else?" Kirk asked in a **shrill** voice.

"Well," Luke said weakly, before slumping down in his chair.

Chapter 18: Spelling High-Frequency Words

"You didn't invite anyone else? What, you didn't have time to text message your friends? I don't understand," Kirk said. Without waiting for Luke to reply, he continued **crossly**. "I'm going to have to tell Max we don't have two teams now."

✶ ✶ ✶ ✶ ✶ ✶ ✶ ✶ ✶ ✶

crossly– *irritably*

✶ ✶ ✶ ✶ ✶ ✶ ✶ ✶ ✶ ✶

"Kirk, I don't understand why you're angry with Luke that his friend can't play," the king said.

"That's just it!" Kirk said loudly. "He doesn't even know if his friends can play because he hasn't asked them. Isn't that right, Luke?"

Luke's face reddened. "I called Jimmy. He didn't answer. I called a couple more friends and they didn't answer, either," he said, defending himself.

"But did you message them? We told you that kids don't answer the phone," Kirk asked.

"Yes, and I said that was rude," the queen said, remembering.

"I, I," Luke stuttered. "No, I didn't," he admitted, hanging his head.

"You don't want to play? Why didn't you just say so?" Kirk asked, rolling his eyes.

"I *do* want to play!" Luke shouted as tears threatened. "I just, I don't want to send text messages."

"Why not?" Ellen asked.

He hesitated and then sighed. "Because I don't want to misspell anything. They'll make fun of me," he said, lip trembling.

"But your spelling has improved a lot!" the queen said.

"It hasn't kept me from making mistakes. I'm sorry, Kirk. I could have asked you to message my friends for me," Luke said.

"Not very nice friends if they make fun of you for spelling mistakes," Ellen said.

"That's how guys are," Kirk admitted. "Give me your communicator, Luke, and I'll message Jimmy for you. If he doesn't respond right away, we'll message some other friends. We should be able to find someone to play."

"I don't think this is a good solution," the king said. When the boys asked why, he explained. "Luke, you need to be confident enough in your spelling to send your own text messages."

"I've learned a lot of spelling strategies already," Luke said.

"That is true. But I'm now realizing that we haven't had you focused on learning the words we use most."

94

Chapter 18: Spelling High-Frequency Words

The king called for *The Guide to Grammar Galaxy* to be brought to him. When it arrived, he read the article on spelling high-frequency words.

Spelling High-Frequency Words
One strategy for improving spelling is to memorize the spelling of words that are commonly misspelled.
Another effective strategy is to memorize the spelling of the most frequently used words. The Fry Word List was compiled by Dr. Edwin Fry. It is a list of the 1,000 most-used words in reading material from grades 3-9. Knowing these words would allow someone to read 90% of books and other reading material.
Combining these strategies produces a list of just 35 words that should be a particular focus for spelling practice. Use phonics, spelling rules, copywork, dictation, and mnemonic approaches to learn the spelling of the words in the chart below.

against	different	friend	probably	surprise
already	disease	government	receive	until
because	doesn't	instead	remember	weight
beginning	enough	million	rhythm	
believe	especially	necessary	separate	
business	exciting	notice	similar	
chief	experience	opposite	straight	
dictionary	finally	particular	studying	

"Just 35 words?" Luke said, marveling.

"Yes, just 35 words to focus on. Of course, you may not remember how to spell some of the other 900-plus words. But this list is a good place to start," the king said.

"Luke, this list is so small, you could save a copy of it on your communicator. Then you could check your spelling in your messages before you send them," Ellen said.

"That's a good idea!" Luke said. "Could I look at the list while I message Jimmy?" he asked his father.

"Of course!" the king answered. "I hope he can join you for laser tag. But while you wait for the boys to arrive, would you send out a mission on spelling high-frequency words? I know you're not the only one who isn't confident in spelling, Luke."

The three children agreed and asked Screen to help them create and send the mission.

What does *shrill* mean?

What is the Fry Word List?

Why didn't Luke want to text message his friends?

Unit IV: Adventures in Grammar

Chapter 19

The queen walked into the king's office and asked Screen to play breaking news. "You need to see this," she said in a serious tone.

The king could see picketers carrying signs. They were marching around the Parliament buildings, chanting. A reporter described the scene and then interviewed a picketer.

"Our grammar is terrible, and it's clear why. We don't teach diagramming anymore," a woman said angrily. Several people behind her shouted their approval. "I learned diagramming, and all of these people did, too. But our kids? No." Several protesters applauded.

"There you have it," the reporter said. "These people are demanding that diagramming be a requirement for all school children."

The king's mouth fell open. "A requirement?" he roared. "That's preposterous!"

"Dear, we both learned sentence diagramming," the queen said sweetly. "And we have excellent grammar."

"We have excellent grammar, but I don't think diagramming has anything to do with it. Did you *like* diagramming? I hated it!" he declared, still **irked** by the protesting.

✯ ✯ ✯ ✯ ✯ ✯ ✯ ✯ ✯

irked – *annoyed*
shady – *dishonest*
concession – *deal*

✯ ✯ ✯ ✯ ✯ ✯ ✯ ✯ ✯

"I didn't mind it. Perhaps our children's grammar would be better if we taught diagramming," she suggested.

"The main reason children struggle with grammar is the Gremlin, plain and simple. He is probably paying these people to protest through one of his many **shady** organizations. Who protests for diagramming? It makes no sense!" The king began pacing. "I need to talk with the Prime Minister. Thank you for bringing this to my attention," he told his wife. She left to give him privacy for his call.

When the Prime Minister was on the screen, he told the king he had been expecting the call.

"These people can't be serious about requiring diagramming," the king began.

"I'm afraid they are, Your Highness. We keep having grammar problems in the galaxy. And the people believe that teaching diagramming would solve them," the Prime Minister said.

"I think requiring diagramming goes too far. Our young people can learn grammar without it," the king said.

"I understand, Your Majesty. But these protesters are going to require some type of **concession**."

"What do you propose?"

"We could give diagramming a special focus each year. We can call it Diagramming Week. We can use the week to teach diagramming to all students. Teachers who enjoy teaching it could continue to do so. But they wouldn't be required to keep teaching it."

"I like it!" the king said, stroking his beard. "Almost like Shark Week," he said.

The Prime Minister seemed surprised but agreed. "Yes, yes, a little like Shark Week."

"All right. I will make an immediate declaration. In fact, I'll teach diagramming to the whole planet via video."

"Splendid idea, Sire," the Prime Minister said. The two said their goodbyes.

The king later explained the idea to the queen and she loved it. "I can't wait to see you teach it," she said.

"Yes," the king said slowly. "There's just one problem."

"What's that?"

"I can't remember anything about diagramming," he admitted.

The queen giggled. "I suppose you'll have to study. I'm sure the guidebook can help," she suggested.

"Yes! Of course!" the king replied, pleased with the suggestion. He excused himself and made his way to the castle library. He found *The Guide to Grammar Galaxy* and located the article on diagramming sentences.

Diagramming Sentences
Diagramming a sentence allows the visualization of its parts. You must know the parts of speech in a sentence to create the diagram. Review them and then you are ready to learn how to diagram. There are diagramming rules for every part of speech and every sentence type. But these are the basics.

Chapter 19: Diagramming Sentences

1. **Simple subject and predicate**
Josie chewed.

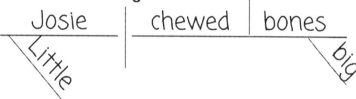

Subject and predicate go on the horizontal line, separated by a vertical line.

2. **Direct object**
Josie chewed bones.

Direct object follows verb on horizontal line, separated by a top vertical line.

3. **Adjective**
Little Josie chewed big bones.

Adjectives are written on slanted lines under the nouns they modify.

4. **Adverb**
Little Josie quickly chewed big bones.

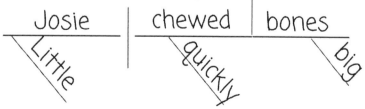

Adverbs are written on slanted lines under the verbs they modify.

"This isn't as complicated as I remembered," the king thought aloud. He did a little more research and then planned a presentation for Diagramming Week. He asked his head programmer for help because he wanted to show slides. The programmer said it would be no problem.

The king had arranged for a crew to come to his office to film the live presentation. The queen made sure his beard was trimmed and his suit was pressed. He didn't feel nervous and the slides appeared on screen as they should. After he was finished, the royal family congratulated him on a fine presentation. The king waited to see the reaction in the paper the next day.

The headline read "King Demands Diagramming." The king grew more and more upset as he read the article. "Why are we returning to these old-fashioned methods of learning grammar?" one woman, who was quoted in the article, complained.

"I hated diagramming and now it's required?" another man had said after watching the king's presentation.

"Dear, you'll never make all the people happy," the queen said, rubbing his back.

"I know, but where are all the protesters? They should be happy about this," he said, putting the paper down in disgust.

"Do *you* think it's a good idea for children to learn diagramming?" the queen asked him.

"Do I? Hm. I didn't think so at first. But now I think it could help visual learners understand grammar better," he said. He smiled at his wife. "I know what you're going to say. If I think it's a good idea, I shouldn't worry about what other people think."

"Exactly! Let's have the children get to work on a diagramming mission. If they express enthusiasm for it, the other young people will be willing to give it a try," the queen said.

"I don't remember everything about diagramming. But I remember why I married you," the king said, kissing her warmly.

Chapter 19: Diagramming Sentences

What is a concession?

What must you know first to diagram a sentence?

Why was the king upset about the newspaper article?

Chapter 20

The English family was expecting guests one Saturday evening. The queen **bustled** around, directing the family to do chores.

★★★★★★★★★★
bustled – *scurried*
amenable – *agreeable*
ire – *anger*
★★★★★★★★★★

"Get the feather duster, Luke," she ordered.

"Okay," Luke answered cheerfully. He hoped that being **amenable** would get chores over with sooner.

"Kirk, get the vacuum," she directed.

Kirk was ready to obey when he thought to ask, "Doesn't the robot do the vacuuming?"

The queen thought for a moment and then said, "Get the mop."

Kirk hesitated, thinking about their robot mop. "I'll make sure it's running," he said, leaving swiftly. He didn't want to raise his mother's **ire**.

"Clean the guest toilet," the queen told her husband.

Ellen's eyes grew wide, waiting for her father's response. He paused and thought his wife must have been talking to Ellen. "Yes, Ellen. Clean the guest toilet. I'm going to go tidy up the garden."

The queen was so busy tidying up that she didn't seem to hear him.

Just then, Luke arrived with the feather duster. "Clean the bookshelves," Ellen directed him as she walked to the guest bath.

"Hey!" Luke objected. He didn't need two people giving him orders.

Ellen smirked. "Get started," she said, enjoying the feeling of power.

Kirk returned and reported that the robot mop was cleaning the sunroom.

"Put these things in the storage room," the queen said, handing Kirk several items that didn't belong in the sitting room.

Chapter 20: Grammatical Mood

Kirk knew better than to argue. "Come with me, Comet!" he said to their dog, who happily tagged along.

"Ellen, when you're finished with the bath, clean the sunroom windows," the queen called out.

The rest of the day continued with the queen giving orders to the children. She wanted to make sure the castle was presentable for their guests.

Before dinner that evening, the queen seemed particularly bossy to the staff. The king thought she must be worried about making a bad impression.

Then Luke's manners at dinner were poor. "Give me another piece!" he'd said after finishing his first serving of cake. The king said his name sternly. Perhaps the queen's constant orders had contributed to Luke's behavior, he thought.

All in all, however, the dinner party was pleasant. Their guests left with the king saying, "Come visit us again!"

The children were relieved the guests were gone. Their mother wouldn't be stressed about how things looked.

The whole family was fatigued and went to bed early.

The next morning at breakfast, the king asked his wife how she thought the party had gone.

"How do you think it went?" she responded.

"Are you not wanting to say that you weren't happy with it?" the king asked.

"Are you not wanting to give your opinion of the evening?" she asked, her voice rising.

The king was worried that saying he thought it went well would set his wife off. Instead, he decided to have his children give their opinion. "How do you think it went?" he asked them.

"Why are you asking? Is something wrong?" Kirk asked.

"Is there something you're not telling us?" Ellen asked worriedly.

"Why would you think something was wrong?" the queen asked, frowning.

"What are you all talking about?" Luke asked.

"How did the party go last night? Is that the question?" Ellen asked.

"Why isn't anyone answering the question?" the queen said in frustration.

"Why are you getting so upset?" the king asked her.

"Why do you think I'm upset?" the queen asked, her neck muscles tense.

"Why wouldn't I think that?" the king said, also getting frustrated.

"Why do we all keep asking questions?" Ellen asked.

"What do you mean?" the king asked.

"Why isn't anyone answering the question?" Luke asked.

"Isn't that what I said?" the queen said in a shrill voice.

"Why are you in a bad mood?" the king asked angrily.

Kirk quietly watched his family's discussion for a few moments. Then he interjected to ask Screen, "Is anything happening on planet Sentence today?"

"Are you wanting news from planet Sentence?" Screen responded.

"Do you have news from the planet?" Kirk continued.

"Is this what you were looking for?" Screen asked, showing a report on the number of active sentences. At the top of the report, the mood of the day was listed as interrogative.

The king was staring at the screen. "Why is there a mood of the day?" he asked.

"Are you asking about the new mood of the day feature on the planet?" Screen asked.

"Was this approved by me?" the king asked.

"Are you asking if the feature was approved by you?" Screen asked. A brief news item that explained the grammatical mood of the day was displayed on the screen.

The king read it, then asked Screen, "What was the grammatical mood of the day yesterday?"

"Are you wanting to know that the grammatical mood of yesterday was imperative?" Screen asked.

The king sighed.

"Are you thinking this is the Gremlin's doing?" Kirk asked. The king nodded and motioned for his family to follow him to the castle library. When they arrived, he removed *The Guide to Grammar Galaxy* from the shelf and read them the article on grammatical mood.

Chapter 20: Grammatical Mood

Grammatical Mood

Grammatical mood is used to make the writer's or speaker's intention clear, primarily by the form and tone of the verb. There are five main types of grammatical mood.

1) **Interrogative mood** asks a question and uses helping verb forms of *be*, *do*, *is*, and *have*.

Are you going to camp?
When will you have enough money?

2) **Imperative mood** issues a command, often with the subject *you* understood but not specified.

(You) Grab me a tissue.
When you finish your math, start on your science.

3) **Indicative mood** makes statements of fact or belief.

I worry about kids who ride bikes without helmets.
There are about 100 million stars in the average galaxy.

4) **Conditional mood** is a statement that is dependent on conditions. It includes the helping verbs *would* and *should* and may use the if/then construction.

When we see the movie, we should get some popcorn.
If the concession stand is too busy, then I would skip the popcorn.

5) **Subjunctive mood** expresses a wish for something that may not be possible. The verb can indicate a desire, a suggestion, or a demand that may not be realized. The subjunctive uses the third-person (he, she, they) form of the verb without the -s, and it uses *be* rather than *is/are*. When describing a wish or a possibility, use *were* instead of *was*.

The teacher suggested that the student **seek** outside tutoring.
I desire that the students **be** heard.
If I **were** a millionaire, I'd buy a yacht.

"Are you saying that Mother was in a grammatical mood yesterday?" Luke asked.

"Are you trying to get me into trouble, young man?" the king asked, smirking.

"What are you going to do about the mood of the day on planet English?" the queen asked. The king pretended to cut his throat to indicate that he would end it.

"Do you think other families are having trouble communicating because of the mood of the day?" Ellen asked.

"Are you suggesting that we create a mission on grammatical mood, Ellen?" Kirk asked, smiling.

She didn't bother trying to answer. Instead, she worked together with her brothers to create the mission. Their father contacted the authorities on planet Sentence and asked them to stop the mood of the day. But he didn't know how quickly his order would take effect.

What does *amenable* mean?

How many main types of grammatical mood are there?

What was the grammatical mood of the day when the queen was directing the family to do chores?

Chapter 21

"I can't wait to see the new *Star Journey* movie. How about you, Father?" Luke asked one evening at dinner.

"I am looking forward to it, yes," the king said. "Screen, how much are tickets?" When Screen responded, the king began complaining. "I don't know how they can justify these outrageous prices! I feel I'm encouraging them if I buy tickets."

Luke hung his head in disappointment.

"Dear, we don't go to movies very often, and the children have been looking forward to it," the queen said sweetly.

The king scanned the table to see his children giving him pleading looks. "All right," the king said begrudgingly.

The children cheered.

"I'll handle ordering the tickets," the queen offered. She didn't want him to see the final price and change his mind.

The next week, the royal family watched *Star Journey* at the theater. The king grumbled about the expense of the popcorn. The queen calmed him by reminding him that it was a special treat.

When the movie was over, the king had to admit he was glad they had seen it.

"I knew you'd like it!" Luke exclaimed. "Now to boldly go home is my mission." The family laughed as they made their way out of the theater.

When they arrived home, the king encouraged the children to get ready for bed.

"To boldly sleep is my mission," Kirk joked.

"To boldly read is mine," Ellen said.

The king smiled at them and wished them goodnight.

"I would like to boldly read, too," the queen added.

The king groaned, but he agreed he was up for a little reading before bed as well.

The next morning, Cook asked them all about the movie. When they **lauded** the film, she told them she couldn't wait to see it. "For now, my mission is to boldly go buy more eggs." She smiled at them before excusing herself.

★ ★ ★ ★ ★ ★ ★ ★ ★ ★

lauded – *praised*

★ ★ ★ ★ ★ ★ ★ ★ ★ ★

"To boldly go to the next level in my video game is my mission today," Luke announced with a smirk.

"To boldly go to the shopping mall with Cher is mine," Ellen added.

"To boldly go to the computer lab is mine," Kirk said.

Chapter 21: Infinitives

"Okay. I appreciate that you enjoyed *Star Journey*. And the whole 'to boldly go' thing was funny at first, but that phrase has always annoyed me," the king said.

"Why, dear?" the queen asked him.

"Oh, I don't want to have any conflict with you," the king said, putting her off.

"You're not going to tell me why it annoys you?" the queen asked. She seemed hurt.

"Now, dear, it isn't important. What do you have on your **agenda** for today?" he asked, changing the subject.

★ ★ ★ ★ ★ ★ ★ ★ ★ ★

agenda – *schedule*

endeavor – *effort*

★ ★ ★ ★ ★ ★ ★ ★ ★ ★

"To boldly go get my nails done," she said, holding up her hands for inspection.

"Not you, too," he groaned. "Your nails look fine to me." But he made it clear she could go. "I'll be glad when 'to boldly go' isn't a popular phrase around this house," he said mostly to himself.

Later that day, Cook asked him if was ready for lunch. The king wasn't sure because he planned to work out.

"To eat or not to eat—that is the question," Cook joked.

The king chuckled. "Yes, it is. I think I will wait."

Cook promised to make him something a bit later.

He made his way to his bedchamber to change. He saw the butler who asked what his plans were. When the king explained, the butler replied, "To work out is a worthy **endeavor**."

The king frowned. "Yes, yes it is. It's just a strange way of putting it."

"To heartily work out is a worthy endeavor. Is that better?" the butler asked.

"No, it is not. I mean, of course, working out heartily is better than a wimpy workout, but—" The king thought better of bringing up a grammar issue. "Thank you," he said, dismissing the butler.

The king was muttering to himself as he lifted weights. "I just want to work out. I want to heartily workout, too, but I would never say it that way. This *Star Journey* movie is set to ruin this galaxy's grammar."

He gasped and not from exercising. "What if the movie is not causing us to use infinitives?" he asked himself aloud. "I'm going to boldly go and check with Screen. Ack! Why did I say that?"

He made his way to his study and asked Screen for a status report on planet Sentence. Screen could find nothing of note. "Keep searching!" he commanded as he left the room. He was intent to assemble his family in the castel library. Something was happening with infinitives and they needed to know about it.

"To suddenly be summoned is alarming," Luke announced.
The king sighed.
"Is this about your problem with 'to boldly go'?" the queen asked. "Are you sure this is something you want to really focus on?"
The king sighed again. "Infinitives and particularly split infinitives are not the biggest issues to focus on. But they're still important to understand."
The king read aloud on the topic from *The Guide to Grammar Galaxy*.

Infinitives

An infinitive is a noun, adjective, or adverb that is most commonly a combination of the word *to* and the simple form of the verb.

to eat	I like to eat. (noun, direct object of *like*)
to read	I brought a book to read. (adjective, describes *book*)
to improve	I am studying to improve my vocabulary. (adverb, modifies *studying*)

A **split infinitive** is an adverb placed between *to* and the simple verb. Split infinitives should be avoided in formal writing.

to carefully **put**
to boldly **go**

To correct a split infinitive, place the adverb before or after the infinitive, unless the new word order creates confusion.

Chapter 21: Infinitives

> Carefully, she started **to put** her dolls away.
> We are determined **to go** boldly where no one has gone before.

"To boldly go is a split infinitive?" Kirk asked.

"Yes, and some people like your father get quite upset about them," the queen teased.

"To do nothing about the infinitives isn't an option?" Ellen asked.

"Not for me," the king agreed. "Something is causing us to excessively use, er, to use infinitives excessively. Until I discover the source, I want you children to create a mission on infinitives. Then, whatever the Gremlin is up to, we'll be prepared."

Luke started to speak when the king interrupted. "Please don't say 'to boldly go.'"

Luke laughed and got to work on a mission with his brother and sister. The king went back to his study to determine if Screen had more information for him.

What does *endeavor* mean?

How can you fix a split infinitive?

Why doesn't the king like the phrase 'to boldly go'?

Chapter 22

"Now what is it, dear?" the queen asked her husband one morning as he read the paper.

"What it always is. The progressives in Parliament are going to destroy this galaxy. And apparently, I'm the only one willing to do what it takes to stop them."

"Is there something in particular that is upsetting you?" she asked as sweetly as she could.

"Their whole agenda!" he said gruffly. "They want changes made to grammar and spelling rules. They even want to change the kind of literature we have kids reading."

"Do you think the Gremlin is behind this?"

"He's always working to destroy the English language," he said angrily.

"But is there something specific he is doing now?"

"Oh, I don't know," he said, waving her off. "I just want to read the paper so I know what these fools are up to."

The queen was a little hurt. But she knew better than to talk to her husband about it when he was in this mood. She was hopeful that he would be back to his usual self when he got away from the paper.

That evening, the kids suggested they watch a new quiz show. The king reluctantly agreed. Ellen put Comet on the king's lap before the show started. She hoped petting their dog would calm her father down.

At first, it seemed to work. Their father's attention was soon drawn into answering the grammar questions out loud. He was delighted that he knew all the answers.

But then the show took a commercial break. The ad began playing loudly. "Our language is outdated," an announcer said. A paper with red correction marks appeared on the screen. "English needs to be **accessible**. That means we need fewer rules." A paper with a smiley face and a note reading 'Nice work!' appeared. "A progressive language prepares our children for a better future. Join the movement." Video of a happy crowd giving the camera a thumbs up appeared.

★ ★ ★ ★ ★ ★ ★ ★ ★ ★

accessible – *user-friendly*
impede – *hinder*
usurp – *take*

★ ★ ★ ★ ★ ★ ★ ★ ★ ★

The king's jaw dropped. Then he clenched his fists and stood up, forcing Comet to the floor.

"Dear…" the queen said to try to **impede** the coming explosion.

"Don't tell me to calm down. This is an attempted takeover of this galaxy. They are trying to **usurp** my authority. The progressives have been working against me in an ongoing manner for decades." The king began pacing. "I can't watch this anymore." He left the room in a rush.

"Wow. I don't know if I've seen father that angry before," Ellen said.

"Oh, I have," Luke said. Ellen hushed him.

"He was so upset about the progressives this morning, too. I hope that some sleep will improve his attitude," the queen said.

"Is this the Gremlin's work?" Kirk asked.

"That's what I asked your father. I don't think so. I think it's just the progressives that are upsetting him," the queen answered. "I'm going to go see if I can encourage him. You children are welcome to finish the show before you get ready for bed."

The children nodded and waited until their mother left before they discussed their father's outburst.

"I wish there were something we could do to help," Ellen said.

"Maybe there is," Kirk said.

"What do you mean?" Luke asked.

"I don't know what progressives are all about. Do you?" Kirk asked. When they shook their heads that they did not, he continued. "Let's look it up in the guidebook. Maybe there is something we can do as guardians. It's our job after all."

Ellen and Luke liked the idea and followed their brother to the castle library. Kirk found an article on progressive tense and read it aloud for them.

Chapter 22: Progressive Tense

> Progressive Tense
>
> The progressive tense is used to show that a verb's action is in progress and ongoing. The progressive tense is constructed of the helping verb *be* plus the present participle form of the verb (-ing).
>
> There are six progressive tenses: present, past, future, present perfect, past perfect, and future perfect. The table below compares the progressive tenses to the standard tenses.

Tense	Progressive	Standard
Present	She **is reading** the book.	She **reads** the book.
Past	She **was reading** the book.	She **read** the book.
Future	She **will be reading** the book.	She **will read** the book.
Present Perfect	She **has been reading** the book.	She **has read** the book.
Past Perfect	She **had been reading** the book.	She **had read** the book.
Future Perfect	She **will have been reading** the book.	She **will have read** the book.

"Father said something about the progressives working against him in an ongoing way," Ellen said.

"Right," Kirk said, thinking.

"I don't think we need these progressives, do you?" Luke asked. "The standard tenses get the job done. And if they are upsetting Father so much, why don't we do something about them?"

"Like what?" Ellen asked.

"We could send out a mission asking the guardians to identify them. Then we could go to planet Sentence, find them, and send them to planet Recycling," Luke said.

"Would we talk to Father about it first?" Ellen asked, frowning.

"You saw how upset he was. He works so hard to protect the galaxy. Why don't we do this for him? He will be so relieved," Luke said.

"I don't know…" Kirk said, grimacing. "He didn't ask us to do it."

"Father always says we shouldn't wait to be told to do things, right?" Luke asked.

"Yes," Ellen answered slowly.

Kirk sighed. "Well, it's too late to do anything about it tonight. Let's sleep on it. If we still think it's a good idea tomorrow, we'll send out a mission and make a quick trip to planet Sentence. I would love to be back in time to surprise Father."

His brother and sister agreed on the plan and got ready for bed.

The next morning, the three of them met in the library and reviewed the article in the guidebook again. While their father might not want them to send out a mission without his knowledge, they agreed that he would be happy having his progressive tense problem solved.

They worked together on a mission and used the space porter to travel to planet Sentence. They hoped their father wouldn't notice they were missing.

What does *usurp* mean?

What is unique about the progressive tense?

How do you think the king will react when he learns the children have sent out a progressive tense mission?

Chapter 23

"Where do you think he got all that money?" Ellen whispered to Kirk at dinner one evening.

"What money?" the king interjected without allowing Kirk to answer.

"The money he stole," Ellen answered.

"Who stole money?" the king asked his wife.

"This is the first I've heard of it, dear," the queen said, shrugging.

"Five million dollars!" Luke exclaimed.

"Has this been on the news?" the king asked. "I haven't seen it in the paper."

"No, Father. It's a show," Ellen answered hesitantly.

"What show?"

"It's *TheyDunnit*. It's a new show on GalaxyFlix," she said slowly.

"A new show you three have watched without our knowledge?" the king asked, his voice rising.

The three nodded with their heads down.

"You know how we feel about that," the king said sternly.

"We don't want you watching shows that we haven't approved. If this is a murder mystery show, you could have trouble sleeping," the queen explained.

"You're right," Kirk said. "We should have asked permission."

Chapter 23: Adverbial Clauses & Phrases

"But it doesn't have any violence! The mysteries are nonviolent crimes. It's not an adult show," Ellen interjected.

"I see," the king said. "We still want you to talk with us about shows you're interested in watching."

"Yes. You still need permission. It sounds like something we would enjoy watching as a family," the queen added.

"You'll like it, Mother," Ellen said, smiling in her direction.

"Why don't we watch it this evening?" the queen suggested.

Ellen recommended that her parents watch the first episode before they watched the second one as a family.

The king thought that was a wonderful idea. But he told the children that they would be cleaning the kitchen all week as a consequence of their choice. The three of them knew better than to complain. And they didn't mind helping Cook.

Later the royal couple asked Screen to play the first episode of *TheyDunnit* for them in the media room. After watching, the two agreed it was a fascinating show. The story **depicted** a man who had successfully stolen five million dollars. The man gave the camera crew a tour of the **palatial** home he'd purchased with the money.

✯ ✯ ✯ ✯ ✯ ✯ ✯ ✯ ✯ ✯

depicted – *showed*
palatial – *grand*
intoned – *spoke*

✯ ✯ ✯ ✯ ✯ ✯ ✯ ✯ ✯ ✯

The host asked him if he was afraid of being caught. "Not at all," he said. "To be caught, you would have to determine when, where, and how I stole the money. And I don't think you will," he said with a sly smile at the camera.

"Talk about overconfident!" the king exclaimed.

"He's playing it up for the show," the queen said. "I see why the children like it. I want to figure out how he did it."

"Yes, it's a compelling concept for a show," the king agreed.

The children boisterously entered the media room. Kirk asked his father's permission and then asked Screen to play the second episode of *TheyDunnit*.

The title of the show faded in: "Where the Crime Took Place." The host of the show then appeared on screen with an unfocused background. "I'm here in the place where our criminal stole five million dollars," he **intoned** dramatically. We are going to give you clues that may help you determine the exact location."

The camera zoomed out slightly to show some corn stalks behind him. "That's corn!" Luke said. "Where does corn grow?"

"Not around here," Kirk answered. "May I research this, Father?" he asked.

The king smiled at his children's enthusiasm and agreed.

Kirk used his communicator to search briefly. "I have a map of all the places on the planet where corn grows. And it's a huge area," Kirk groaned.

The host of the show began walking slowly through the rows of corn. He plucked a tassel from a stalk as he went. "This is the general location where our thief got his money. But he didn't find it in a cornfield," he said mischievously. The title "Where the Crime Took Place" faded in again.

"Where the crime took place," Ellen read aloud.

The view then switched to a satellite view of a small town surrounded by fields. The buildings were so small that no details were apparent. The host spoke as the camera slowly zoomed in. "This small town was the scene of a five-million-dollar heist."

The next scene had the host walking down what appeared to be main street. None of the background was in focus. "If we were playing a game of Cold-Warm-Hot to find the location of this crime, I'd be getting hot," the host said, smirking.

"It's a brick building behind him," Ellen said. "People are going in, so it has to be a public place."

"They need to give us more clues!" Luke said.

"After the commercial plays," the queen said.

"After the commercial plays, they'll give us more clues?" Luke said. "I hope so."

"If they don't give us more clues," Ellen said.

"If they don't give us more clues, what?" Luke asked.

Ellen just shrugged.

"Where he was," Kirk said.

"What about where he was?" Luke asked.

Kirk also shrugged.

"As if he would never be caught," the king said.

"Yes? What about it?" Luke asked his father.

The king shrugged.

"Because no one is making sense," Luke said.

The king looked at his youngest son, wide-eyed. "While this show became popular," he said. He didn't wait for a response but spoke to Screen. "If I could have a report from planet Sentence."

"Your Majesty?" Screen responded quizzically at first. Then he assumed the king wanted a report. He said nothing unusal was occurring on the planet. "But *TheyDunnit* is the most popular new show there," he added.

"As the show's popularity increased," the king said to himself. He became agitated and began pacing. "I've got it!" he said.

"You know when, where, and how he did it?" Ellen asked.

The king shook his head and motioned for his family to follow him. He led them to the castle library, where he removed *The Guide to Grammar Galaxy* from its shelf. He scanned the table of contents until he found the article he was looking for. He read it aloud to them.

Adverbial Clauses & Phrases

Adverbial phrases are groups of words that function as adverbs (communicating where, when, how, or why) that don't include both a subject and predicate. They may be prepositional phrases, infinitives, or an adverb pairing.

I can read **in the car**. (prepositional phrase communicating where)

I like reading **to pass the time**. (adverb communicating why)

I like reading mysteries **very quickly**. (adverb pairing communicating how)

Adverbial clauses are dependent clauses that include both a subject and predicate, or these are understood from the sentence.

Some common conjunctions used in adverbial clauses are listed in the chart below.

Communicates	Conjunctions	Example
Where	anywhere, everywhere, where, wherever	I like to read **wherever I find a comfy spot**.
When	after, as long as, before, since, when, while, until	I like to read **before I go to bed**.
How	although, as, if, like, though, unless, while	I read **as quietly as I can if I am up late**.
Why	because, given, in order to, since, so that	I stay up late reading **because I want to finish the book**.

Chapter 23: Adverbial Clauses & Phrases

"If you're saying what I think you're saying," Kirk said.
"Because of the popularity of *TheyDunnit*," the king said.
"Unless we do something," Ellen said.
"On the planet," Luke agreed.

The king wanted to make sure they understood, so he began writing a text to the children's communicators. It read "The show has caused overuse of adverbial clauses and phrases. Send out a mission. I will stop the show from airing on planet Sentence."

The three English children nodded and got to work on a mission called Adverbial Clauses & Phrases.

What does *intoned* mean?

What is the difference between an adverbial clause and phrase?

How do you think the words on planet Sentence will respond when the king stops *TheyDunnit* from airing there?

Chapter 24

The royal family was enjoying a snack in the sunroom when the queen made an announcement. "My cousins are planning a family reunion! I'm so excited," she gushed.

"When is it?" the king asked.

"It's the first weekend of next month."

"The whole weekend?" the king asked, trying to hide his **vexation**.

The queen noticed. "Yes, the whole weekend," she answered **curtly**. "One weekend is not too much to ask to spend with my family, given that we rarely see them." The queen challenged the king to argue with her look.

★★★★★★★★★★

vexation – annoyance

curtly - tersely

★★★★★★★★★★

"Of course not, dear. I look forward to seeing your family," the king said to placate her.

"I should hope so," she said, relaxing a bit. She turned her attention to the kids. "I can't wait for you children to meet my cousins and their families."

"How many cousins do you have, Mother?" Ellen asked.

"The reunion is for my father's side of the family. I believe I have 63 first cousins," she answered.

"You have 63 cousins? Wow! That's a lot!" Luke exclaimed.

"Yes, my father had 12 siblings. It's a big family," the queen explained.

"Do you know them all?" Kirk asked.

The queen looked glum. "I have to admit I don't. I was one of the youngest cousins, so many of my cousins moved away when I was little."

"How will you know who everyone is then?" Luke asked.

"I won't," the queen said sadly.

"I have an idea," Ellen said with enthusiasm. "What if you had all of your cousins send you pictures and tell you about their families before the reunion? You could put all the information together in a scrapbook that people could read."

The queen was quiet.

"You don't have to do that if you don't want to," Ellen said apologetically.

The queen dabbed at tears in the corners of her eyes. "No, I love the idea. I'm just so touched that you suggested it," she said, reaching to hug Ellen. Ellen beamed.

The queen stayed busy putting her cousins' scrapbook together before the reunion. She enjoyed the back-and-forth conversations they had as she worked.

The day they were scheduled to leave for the reunion, she was **disconcerted** by her family's slowness in getting ready. The king advised the children to obey quickly. Seeing his wife's state, he suggested they use the space porter to travel. That way they could spend more time with her family, he explained. The queen cried happy tears and thanked him for his thoughtfulness.

★★★★★★★★★★

disconcerted – perturbed

★★★★★★★★★★

The queen carried a copy of the cousin scrapbook in her hands. She trembled when she saw the crowd that had gathered. She didn't know where to start. But then one of the cousins close to her age approached her and gave her a big hug. She was so enthralled by the conversation that she almost forgot to introduce her family.

"You know my husband, of course," she said, grinning. "This is my daughter, my daughter. This is Ellen, Ellen," she stuttered. She shook her head. "I'm so excited I can't talk straight," she explained with a chuckle. "This is Kirk. Uh. Hm. This Kirk," she said, giving up on what she wanted to say. "And this is my youngest, Luke," she said, relieved that she hadn't stuttered. The children shook the cousin's hand as they were introduced.

"Oh, and this is the scrapbook, the scrapbook. Uh. Here," she said, handing it to her cousin, her face reddening.

"It's so wonderful to have all the family information in one place. You did a beautiful job with it," the queen's cousin said warmly.

Chapter 24: Relative Pronouns

The queen thanked her and after a few more minutes of chatting, she moved to another cousin to visit. Once again, the queen began stuttering as she introduced her family. She looked to her husband in a panic as her cousin looked through the scrapbook. "You're just excited, dear," he whispered to soothe her.

"Yes, yes, you're right," she said quietly, trying to console herself.

The queen pointed to an old photo in the scrapbook and told her cousin, "This is the house, the house. Er. This is the house." Her shoulders sagged as she felt she was making a fool of herself.

"Our fathers grew up there," her cousin suggested.

"Yes!" the queen said with relief.

She visited with a third cousin and had similar problems communicating. "Maybe we should go," she told her husband as she walked away.

"You can't be serious!" the king said. "You'll calm down. You're just excited. You'll regret not visiting with your cousins," he told her.

Luke approached the couple, waving a soda in his hand. "This is the soda. This is the soda. This is the soda. See?" he said, showing it to them.

The king and queen looked at one another and said, "Something is wrong," in unison.

"Don't worry," the king said. "I'll get to the bottom of it." He stepped away from the group and contacted Screen via communicator. "Is anything unusual happening on planet Sentence?" he asked.

"Nothing unusual, Sire. No protests or new laws. There *is* a big family reunion," Screen replied.

"A family reunion?"

"Yes, relative pronouns were invited to a family reunion picnic. It seems to be a peaceful gathering."

"Thank you," the king said.

He then gathered Kirk, Luke, and Ellen and explained that the Gremlin had caused another crisis. By occupying relative pronouns at a family reunion, he had made them unavailable on planet English. The king asked his children to do three things: 1) use the space porter to return home, 2) look up relative pronouns in the guidebook, and 3) send out a mission to the guardians.

He said he planned to have Grammar Patrol break up the planet Sentence picnic because the picnic grounds hadn't been reserved.

"They'll be disappointed that the picnic is over," Luke said.

"Yes, but your mother will be even more disappointed if we don't get relative pronouns back to work," the king replied.

Luke agreed and returned to the castle with his brother and sister. They quickly found an article on relative pronouns in the guidebook and read it together.

Relative Pronouns

A relative pronoun begins an adjective clause. An adjective clause is a dependent or subordinate clause, providing more information about a noun (also called the antecedent). The most common relative pronouns are *that, which, who, whose,* and *whom*. The pronouns *that* and *which* are <u>not</u> used to refer to people.

This is the book that got Joe interested in reading.
The clause beginning with <u>that</u> describes <u>book</u>.

She is the librarian who told me about this series.
The clause beginning with <u>who</u> describes <u>librarian</u>.

If the adjective clause is not essential in identification or to the sentence's meaning, it is set apart with commas. *If we know specifically who or what without the clause, it is nonessential. <u>That</u> is always used to introduce an essential clause.*

Natalie, who wears her hair in pigtails, likes reading picture books. (not essential)
Books that include new vocabulary words improving reading skills. (essential)

"I was trying to tell Mother and Father about the soda they had at the reunion and I couldn't. Now I know why," Luke said.

"We need to hurry and send out a mission," Ellen said. "Mother needs relative pronouns to enjoy the reunion."

Her brothers agreed and the three of them sent a mission. They hoped the guardians could help Grammar Patrol identify relative pronouns attending the planet Sentence reunion.

Chapter 24: Relative Pronouns

What does *vexation* mean?

What are some examples of relative pronouns?

Why was the queen stuttering at the reunion?

Chapter 25

The king and queen were in the media room when the king asked Screen to show the evening news. The queen frowned but said nothing.

"A new poll suggests that the king's approval ratings have dropped to an all-time low," the news anchor said.

The king's face reddened.

"Now, dear, this is why I told you to stop watching the news," the queen said.

Chapter 25: Misplaced Modifiers

"I have to know what's happening in the galaxy," the king said, hushing her so he could continue listening.

The news story had shifted to interviews with citizens. "He seems to have a lot of free time," one man said. "More than I have!"

A reporter asked a little girl her opinion of the king. "My mother says he eats too many sweets," she said, patting her belly.

The king was aghast.

"Dear, let's turn this off," the queen urged him.

Another man being interviewed said, "They say the Gremlin is a bad guy, but honestly, I don't know who's worse."

The king gasped. "He doesn't know if I'm any better than the Gremlin? This is preposterous!" He jumped up and began pacing.

"I know that look. What are you going to do?" the queen asked.

"I'm going to hire a public relations expert. I have to change the public's **perception** of me," he said resolutely.

✶ ✶ ✶ ✶ ✶ ✶ ✶ ✶ ✶ ✶

perception – opinion
animatedly – energetically

✶ ✶ ✶ ✶ ✶ ✶ ✶ ✶ ✶ ✶

"I'm so glad you're being proactive instead of sulking."

The king gave her a warning glance.

"I mean, I think that's a great plan," she said, correcting herself.

The king nodded. "I don't think I have too many desserts. I enjoy them, but I work out. You don't think I eat too many desserts, do you?" he asked.

The queen hesitated.

"That's just great!" the king complained without waiting for her answer. "I'm fat and no one likes me."

"I think you're wonderful just the way you are," the queen said sweetly.

The king gave her a weak thanks and excused himself.

The next day, the queen was happy to see her husband actively working on the problem.

He was talking on his communicator in a loud voice. "That's a splendid idea. We can have a camera crew filming my day. The people will see me exercising and working hard to protect the galaxy. Thank you!"

Chapter 25: Misplaced Modifiers

When he finished his call, he spoke **animatedly** with the queen about his plan. The magazine *Galaxy Life* had agreed to do a feature article on him, sharing an inside look at his life with the people. The queen nodded and told her husband she was so happy to see him feeling better about things. He said was hopeful that the journalist doing the story would show him in a **favorable** light.

favorable – positive

After spending an intensive day with *Galaxy Life* staff, the king thought he had made a good impression on them. He was eager to get a copy of the article when it was finished. He was even more eager to see his approval ratings go up.

Some weeks later, when the copies featuring the king on the cover arrived, the king gathered everyone around to look at the article.

"I love the photos!" the queen gushed. "You look so handsome."

The king blushed slightly. "You are my favorite queen for a reason," he joked. "It's a long article, so I'm not going to read it aloud."

"We'll leave you alone with it then," the queen said. "Congratulations!" She kissed him on the cheek and ushered the rest of the family out of the sitting room.

The king read the article, smiling as he did so, until he read a troubling sentence: "Constantly making evil plans, the king's daily goal is to defeat the Gremlin." Shrugging it off as a simple mistake, the king continued reading.

"The heavy king's workout gives him the energy he needs for his day," he read. He gasped.

"What are they saying?" he said aloud. He continued reading.

"The castle cook served eggs to the king with large rolls." The king gasped again. He began skimming the article. "The king said after a long nap he would have a busy day."

"I've had enough!" he said in disgust. "This misplaced writer has the worst modifiers ever." He thought for a moment about what he'd said. Then he asked Screen for a status report on planet Sentence.

"With no experience, the governor of planet Sentence recently replaced sentence coordinators," Screen said.

Chapter 25: Misplaced Modifiers

"I think I know what you mean," the king said. He immediately called for his three children to join him in the castle library.

When they arrived, he explained that the *Galaxy Life* article about him was confusing because of misplaced modifiers. He read them the related article from *The Guide to Grammar Galaxy*.

Misplaced Modifiers

Words, phrases, or clauses that are separated from the word they explain can result in an uncertain meaning. These are called misplaced modifiers. Correcting them involves moving the modifier, so it is next to the word it modifies.

A misplaced modifier may be an adjective.

She found an expensive woman's shirt at the thrift store. – *misplaced; the woman isn't expensive.*

She found a woman's expensive shirt at the thrift store. – *correct*

Misplaced modifiers can be adverbs.

She opened the gift they gave her slowly. – *misplaced; they didn't give her the gift slowly.*

She slowly opened the gift they gave her. – *correct*

Misplaced modifiers can be phrases or clauses.

The boy put the hot dog in the trash he had eaten. – *incorrect; the boy hadn't eaten the trash.*

The boy put the hot dog he had eaten in the trash. – *correct*

The child held a snake in his room made of clay. – *incorrect, the room isn't made of clay.*

In his room, the child held a snake made of clay. – *correct*

Dangling modifiers (also called dangling participles) are -ing verbs that often come at the beginning of sentences. They cannot be corrected simply by moving them in the sentence. To correct them, either add the word being modified or change the dangling modifier to a subordinate clause.

Looking around the library, new books were everywhere. – *incorrect; the new books weren't looking around.*

Looking around the library, I saw new books everywhere. – *correct, added the word being modified (I).*

Rotting in the basement, my brother brought up a case of apples. – *incorrect; your brother wasn't rotting in the basement.*

Chapter 25: Misplaced Modifiers

> My brother brought up a case of apples that he found rotting in the basement.
> – *correct; added a subordinate clause.*

"I think it's funnier that my brother was rotting in the basement. You'd be a zombie, Kirk," Luke said. He stretched out his arms in front of him and began moaning and lurching from side to side.

"Hilarious," the king said sarcastically. "We don't have time for clowning around. I'm going to call the governor of planet Sentence and have her reinstate the original sentence coordinators. But you three have to move misplaced modifiers. Send out a mission and then travel to planet Sentence."

"It's a hot guardians' mess," Luke said, agreeing.

"Help him," the king said, groaning.

The three English children got to work creating a mission called Misplaced Modifiers.

What does *favorable* mean?

Why is "hot guardians' mess" a misplaced modifier?

Was the *Galaxy Life* article likely to improve the king's approval rating?

Chapter 26

The king had just finished his State of the Galaxy address. He **steeled** himself to meet with the press afterward. There was always at least one reporter who seemed to be working for the Gremlin. He wasn't looking forward to the questions designed to make him look ineffective.

★ ★ ★ ★ ★ ★ ★ ★ ★

steeled – *strengthened*
splendid – *wonderful*
vied – *competed*

★ ★ ★ ★ ★ ★ ★ ★ ★

The king smiled, took a deep breath, and called on the first reporter. "You feel the guardians are doing an adequate job protecting the English language?" the reporter asked.

"No," the king answered loudly. A hush fell over the press corps. "I think they're doing a **splendid** job," he said, flashing them a toothy grin. The other reporters **vied** for the chance to ask the next question.

"You said that Diagramming Week was a success. Why aren't you having students diagram every week?" a woman asked.

"Diagramming is helpful for some students who need to visualize grammar. If those students want to diagram every week, they should. But we will not be requiring it. Next question," he said, scanning the room. He called on a man in front.

"Yes, did you say that one of our biggest grammar challenges is run-on sentences?" the reporter asked.

"I did indeed," the king answered.

"I know you mentioned our current approach to correcting them. But I'm wondering why you haven't mentioned dashes and parentheses. In the information age, couldn't these punctuation marks allow us to add more information to sentences without creating run-ons?" He held his pen in the air, waiting for the king's response.

The king hesitated. He wasn't sure how it could be a trick question, so he agreed. "Those punctuation marks are another way of preventing run-on sentences, yes," the king said.

"So, Your Highness, may I quote you as saying that you are in favor of using these punctuation marks?" he asked.

"Yes," the king said dismissively.

The press conference continued without many challenging questions, and the king was pleased with how it went. He was even more pleased when his publicity agent told him that the speech had improved his approval ratings.

The next morning, the king was eager to read the paper's perspective on his speech. He was surprised by the headline: "King Supports Use of Punctuation to Defeat Run-On Sentences."

The article defined a run-on sentence as two independent clauses that are incorrectly connected. It explained that the galaxy's prior approach had been to use periods to separate them or to add a comma with a coordinating conjunction.

But with the king's new directive on the use of punctuation, the article continued, planet Sentence's leaders were scrambling. They had to find more dashes and parentheses to meet higher demand.

"What?" the king said out loud. "I didn't give a new directive. And why do we need any more of these punctuation marks than we did before? I've been duped." He put his head in his hands.

"I hate to ask," the queen said.

The king sighed. "Yes, once again I fell for a question designed to trip me up. When will I learn?" He proceeded to explain what had happened.

"What are you going to do?" she asked sympathetically.

He thought for a moment. "I have phone calls to make. I'm going to call the punctuation director on planet Sentence and let her know that we do not need more of these marks. Then I'm going to call the paper and ask a reporter to do a follow-up interview. That way I can clear up the confusion. Most importantly, I'm going to ask the guardians to help. They can help the sentence coordinators determine when these punctuation marks are appropriate."

"I think that's a wonderful idea, dear," the queen said.

When the children came to breakfast, the king explained the problem to them. He then read what *The Guide to Grammar Galaxy* had to say about dashes and parentheses.

Chapter 26: Dashes & Parentheses

Dashes

The dash is a horizontal line used to separate groups of words, unlike the hyphen that is used to separate individual words. Two common dashes are the en dash and the em dash.

The en dash is shorter (like the size of an *N*). It is used to show a range.
I have read 15–20 pages.
The war lasted from 1914–1918.

The em dash is longer (like the size of an *M*). It is used to replace parentheses, colons, and missing information. The em dash can emphasize words and give writing a more casual feel.
I spend a lot of time in the library (usually in the mystery and biography sections).
I spend a lot of time in the library—usually in the mystery and biography sections.
I love two genres of books: mysteries and biographies.
I love two genres of books—mysteries and biographies.
I checked out a book with the faded title: My——ery Island.

Parentheses

Parentheses ( ) are used to enclose nonessential or extra information. Follow these rules for using parentheses.

1. Use a complete sentence or dependent clause if parentheses are not needed.
I rode my bike to the library (after I stopped at my friend's house). - incorrect
After I stopped at my friend's house, I rode my bike to the library. - correct

2. Use punctuation inside the parentheses if it is a complete sentence or requires different punctuation than the main sentence.
I heard my mother say she wanted me to mow the lawn (or did I?) before I left.
My mother asked me to mow the lawn before I left. (I wasn't sure I heard that.)

3. Use commas, colons, and semicolons outside the closing parenthesis.
When she asked me if I had mowed the lawn (louder this time), I had to admit I had not.

"You want us to go to planet Sentence?" Luke asked. Before the king answered, he leaned over to Kirk, cupping his hand over his mouth. "I'm pretty sure he does," he whispered.

"Luke, what you just did with your hand should remind you of what parentheses are used for. They share information on the side," the king said. "But just to be clear. Doing that in conversation is rude."

"Sorry," Luke said, bowing his head.

"Forgiven. I would like you three to leave for planet Sentence immediately. The sentence coordinators are expecting you. Help them sort out when and how to use dashes and parentheses. I don't want them to feel any pressure to use them more often," the king explained.

"But first we send a mission?" Ellen asked.

"Exactly. Thank the guardians in advance for their help. I have some calls to make."

Kirk, Luke, and Ellen got to work on a mission called Dashes and Parentheses.

What does *steeled* mean?

What is the difference between an en and em dash?

Will using more dashes and parentheses prevent run-on sentences?

Unit V: Adventures in Composition & Speaking

Chapter 27

The royal English family was excited about the Galaxy Gymnastics Championships they were attending. The king had suggested that the family learn more about the competitors before the event.

Luke called his family's attention to the men's vault competition. "He is the best in the galaxy at this event," Luke said proudly. The audience gasped at the gymnast's speed, height, and stable landing. "He got almost a perfect score. He'll be hard to beat," Luke said. The rest of the family nodded.

On the other side of the gym, the women's floor competition was ongoing. "That's my favorite," Ellen said. "I love the music. I wish I could flip like that!"

"It requires hours of practice," the queen said.

Ellen nodded in agreement. "This team almost always wins the floor exercise," she went on to explain. The family watched the routine with interest. They clapped along with the music and agreed that it was going to be a tough routine to beat.

Ellen asked her mother if she could start learning gymnastics. The queen explained that she would have to **sacrifice** another activity first. "I understand that it's not only time consuming but expensive," the queen said.

★★★★★★★★★★
sacrifice – *give up*
★★★★★★★★★★

"Expensive? I'm not in favor then," the king said, only half attending to the conversation.

Chapter 27: Parallel Structure

Ellen pouted, then hoped the rest of the competition would change her parents' minds.

"Look!" the queen said, pointing. "They're starting the men's parallel bars. I'm amazed by how quickly and effortlessly they move."

The rest of the family agreed. They watched a young man mount the bars and extend into a handstand. He began a giant swing backward. He did a half twist and flip forward, intending to land with his upper arms on the bar. But he rotated too far forward, slipped through the bars and hit the floor face first. He didn't get up.

His trainer rushed over to him, examined him, and called for an ambulance. "Oh, no!" the queen cried. "His poor mother must be so worried."

A woman came running from the stands to attend to him. "That must be his mother there," Ellen said. The queen nodded. "I hope he'll be okay," Ellen added.

"We all do," the queen replied, noting how everyone's attention was drawn to the young man lying still on the mat.

★ ★ ★ ★ ★ ★ ★ ★ ★ ★

subdued – *quiet*

stay – *stop*

★ ★ ★ ★ ★ ★ ★ ★ ★ ★

The accident had the audience **subdued** for the rest of the competition. But the events were completed as scheduled.

That evening, the king requested that Screen play the news. The gymnast's accident was the lead story. "This promising young gymnast has suffered a severe neck injury. Doctors aren't yet sure if he will compete or even walk again."

The queen gasped and tears started. "That poor young man," she said.

"The head of the Galaxy Gymnastics Association is calling for an immediate **stay** on parallel bars competition until its safety is proven," the news anchor said.

"What do you think of that decision, dear?" the queen asked her husband.

"Possibly an overreaction, but I understand. We want to keep our kids safe. I would be devastated if Ellen suffered that injury."

The queen nodded and dabbed her eyes with a tissue.

The next morning the king was reading his paper and began complaining about the writing.

"Dear, those poor journalists will never be able to write to your standards," the queen said, mildly chastising him.

"My standards aren't that high! How can we expect our young people to write well if paid writers don't?" the king argued.

The queen sighed. "What is it this time? Please tell me it's not commas. Those are so subjective."

"It's not commas. Listen to this. 'The Galaxy Gymnastics Association has determined that the speed, height, and the boys are using the bars with no spotter put athletes at risk of accidents.' Does that sound right to you?"

"Well, they do have a lot of speed and height and I didn't see anyone spotting the poor young man who fell," the queen replied thoughtfully.

"That's not what I meant," the king said. "There's no parallel structure in that."

"Well, there won't be parallel bars in future competitions, it sounds like," the queen agreed.

"You're not understanding. Here's another one," the king said, reading from the article again. "'These athletes are still developing, spend long hours training, and young. That puts them at risk of serious injury.'"

"Yes. You don't agree?" the queen asked, eyebrows raised.

"It's not a matter of agreeing or not. Doesn't that sound terrible?"

"I think the amount of hours they work these young men is too much," the queen said firmly.

The king sighed. "I'm going to talk to the children about this."

"So you've decided not to let Ellen do gymnastics without even getting my opinion?" the queen asked, her voice rising.

"Dear, I love you. I will always get your opinion on things that affect our children," the king said with forced patience.

"That's why I love you, too," the queen said sweetly.

The king turned his attention back to the paper. "Of course," he said with sudden insight. "Not even the *Grammar Gazette* is this bad." He looked up and asked Screen to give him a status report on planet Sentence.

"The top story on planet Sentence is the ban on parallel structure until its safety has been determined," Screen said.

Chapter 27: Parallel Structure

The king laughed despite his earlier annoyance. "Good one, Gremlin." He called for *The Guide to Grammar Galaxy* and explained the problem to the queen.

When the children came to the dining room for breakfast, he read them the article on parallel structure.

Parallel Structure

Parallel structure, also known as parallelism, requires using the same grammatical composition in a sentence. Parallel structure makes sentences easier to read and understand.

Susan enjoys games, crafts, and to read. – incorrect; the list of direct objects includes two nouns and an infinitive.

Susan enjoys games, crafts, and books. – correct; the list of direct objects includes three nouns.

Susan likes to play games, do crafts, and read books. – correct; the list includes verbs and direct objects.

His favorite trips were flying to Disney World, cruising to the Bahamas, and canoeing. – incorrect; canoeing (unlike flying and cruising) does not include a prepositional phrase beginning with *to*.

His favorite trips were flying to Disney World, cruising to the Bahamas, and canoeing to the Adirondacks. – correct; *to the Adirondacks* was added to make the structure parallel.

"Parallel structure has been banned because of the gymnast's accident," the king explained.

"That doesn't make sense," Kirk said.

"It does for the Gremlin. He takes any opportunity to lie, confuse, and to cause problems," the king said.

"What you said wasn't parallel," Kirk said.

The king sighed. "It's affecting our speech, too. I need you three to create a mission on parallel structure. It's not gymnastics, Ellen, but I need your help. You and your brothers will have to go to planet Sentence to correct sentence structure."

Ellen nodded. The king left to have the ban on parallelism lifted. And the three English children worked on a mission called Parallel Structure.

Chapter 27: Parallel Structure

What does *subdued* mean?

Why does parallelism matter?

Why is this sentence not parallel? *He takes any opportunity to lie, confuse, and to cause problems.*

Chapter 28

The queen walked into the kitchen, sniffing as she entered. "What smells delectable? Have you made my favorite chocolate-chip banana muffins, Cook?" she called.

Cook had been sitting by a window with a cup of tea, but she jumped up abruptly. "Yes, yes, I wanted to surprise you."

"You did, my friend. But it looks like I surprised you, too," she said warmly. She made her way to the table where Cook had been sitting. "What were you up to?" she asked, gesturing toward the journal and pen lying there. "Creating new recipes?"

"No. I was doing my morning pages," she answered.

"What are morning pages?" the queen asked.

"I read the book *The Artist's Way* by Julia Cameron and she recommended doing them. I'm not an artist by any means. But it helps me to get my thoughts on paper. And I thought I might want to write a children's book one day," Cook said in a rush. She reddened a little as she realized what she'd admitted to. "Of course, I don't expect to be a best-selling author. Nothing like that. It's just for fun really," she said awkwardly.

"Cook, I think that's wonderful!" the queen gushed.

"You do?" Cook responded in surprise.

"Of course! You have such a way with children. I can see you writing for them. But tell me more about morning pages," the queen said, pouring herself a cup of tea. She sat down across from where Cook had her journal.

Cook beamed. She was excited to talk about her new **pastime**. "Do you keep a journal?" she asked the queen.

"Not **consistently**," the queen admitted.

★★★★★★★★★★

pastime – *hobby*
consistently – *regularly*
★★★★★★★★★★

"I wasn't consistent, either," Cook said. "But that's because I thought there were rules for what to write. I thought I had to write about what happened each day. It also thought it had to be compelling, so I wasn't going to write I served for dinner." She laughed and the queen joined her.

"Then I learned that morning pages can be any writing. There are no rules. It's stream-of-**consciousness** writing. So, I write whatever I'm thinking about."

★ ★ ★ ★ ★ ★ ★ ★ ★

consciousness – *awareness*

★ ★ ★ ★ ★ ★ ★ ★ ★

"But right now I'm thinking about everything I have to do today," the queen said.

"Exactly! You would write that," Cook replied.

"Won't my journal look like a to-do list then?" the queen asked.

"No, because some days you will have ideas for your novel. And other days you will write about something that you're worried about."

"Hm. How much do you have to write?"

"Three pages by hand."

"Isn't that hard to do some days? I know you're busy like I am," the queen said.

"Yes. But when I make myself keep writing, I get some of my best ideas," Cook responded, eyes shining.

"You're convincing me to give morning pages a try," the queen said, smiling at her friend.

"You should!"

"I can't wait to read your children's book one day," the queen said, patting Cook's hand.

"If I keep doing my morning pages, I think I'll have the confidence to start soon," Cook said.

The queen finished her tea and a muffin as she continued visiting. Then she had an idea. "Do you think morning pages would work for children, too?" she asked Cook.

"I don't see why not!"

"Would you be willing to talk to the children about morning pages? Your enthusiasm for writing is likely to sell them on the idea," the queen asked.

"Of course!" Cook said. "It would be a pleasure."

After breakfast, the queen explained to Kirk, Luke, and Ellen that Cook had a new habit she wanted to talk with them about.

Chapter 28: Morning Pages

"I hope she has a habit of making chocolate-chip banana muffins!" Luke joked.

"I do, too," the queen quipped in return. "But this habit could help you become better writers."

The children were curious and went to the kitchen to talk with Cook. They thanked her for the delicious breakfast and asked her about her new habit.

Cook explained that writing first thing in the morning was helping her to become a better, more confident writer. She said a side benefit was that she was able to think through problems on paper. She found herself feeling happier after writing.

"So, how much do you have to type?" Luke asked.

"Oh, you don't type them, Luke. Writing by hand in a journal with a good pen is an important part of the process."

Luke grimaced. "By hand? Ack. So, do you write a paragraph then?"

Cook chuckled. "Yes, by hand. And you write three pages."

"Three pages!" Luke was aghast.

Ellen gave Luke a corrective look and said, "If your journal is small, that's not that much. My question is about mornings. Sometimes I can't write first thing in the morning. Is that the only time you can write?"

"Not at all. Sometimes I write in the afternoon or evening if I'm busy in the morning. But I have made a habit of writing three pages each day," Cook said.

"Three pages," Luke sighed. The rest of them laughed.

"Luke, I encourage you to give it a try. You may like it as much as I do," Cook said.

"I'm not counting on that, but I'll try," Luke said.

That afternoon, the children found notebooks to use as journals. They put them and a pen on their dressers, so they would remember to write in the morning.

At breakfast the next day, Ellen was excited to report that she had completed her morning pages. Kirk had, too. Kirk said he was surprised that it helped him think through a programming problem he was having. Luke stayed quiet.

"Luke, how did your morning pages go?" the queen asked.

"Uh, I forgot to do them," he said, looking down at his lap.

"Whether you forgot or you chose not to do them, you'll complete them after breakfast. Then we'll go over what you wrote," the queen said sternly.

Cook came into the dining room. "Excuse me, Your Highness. I hate to interrupt. But I forgot to tell you something important about morning pages. No one else is allowed to read them." The queen raised her eyebrows. "See, if we are worried that someone will read what we're writing, then it will be harder to come up with ideas. We'll worry about being corrected or judged. And we won't be honest," she said earnestly.

"You aren't going to edit my pages?" Luke asked, looking to the queen. When she shook her head no, he said, "Now you tell me!" Everyone laughed.

The three English children wrote morning pages for several days. Then Luke decided he had to talk to his mother. He found her in her study, working on her novel. He knocked quietly.

"Mother?" When she invited him in, he continued. "I wanted to talk with you about morning pages."

"Now, Luke, I know it's a lot of hand-written work for you. But in addition to helping you become more creative, doing them will improve your handwriting speed. I'm not open to having you stop right now. And that's final," she said curtly.

"I wasn't going to ask you to stop doing them," Luke said solemnly.

"You weren't?" The queen was surprised and curious.

"No. I was going to suggest that we send out a mission on morning pages to the guardians."

"You're kidding."

"No. I like doing them."

"You like doing them? Are you trying to get something, young man?" the queen asked, her eyes narrowed.

Luke laughed. "No. I really like doing them. Sometimes it takes me a while to write that much. But sometimes I write a list of things I want to do. I write about things that bug me. And I've even been writing ideas for a graphic novel."

"You have," the queen said, sitting quietly. Her eyes welled up with tears. She stood and hugged her son. "Have I told you how proud I am of you?" she said.

Chapter 28: Morning Pages

The two of them went to find Kirk and Ellen, so they could work together on a mission called Morning Pages.

What is a *pastime*?

Why didn't Cook want the queen to edit Luke's morning pages?

How many pages should you write when completing morning pages?

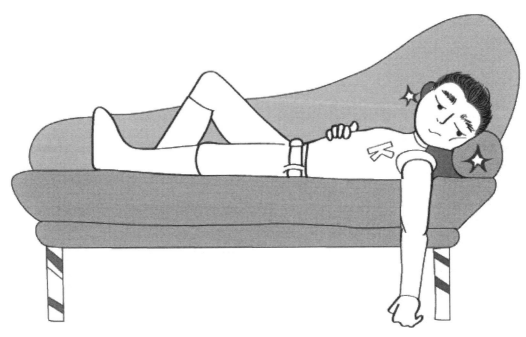

Chapter 29

One morning at breakfast, the king made an announcement. He said he had heard **disturbing** things about the effects of lack of exercise in children. "My children will exercise regularly," he declared.

★ ★ ★ ★ ★ ★ ★ ★ ★ ★
disturbing – *worrying*
★ ★ ★ ★ ★ ★ ★ ★ ★ ★

Kirk, Luke, and Ellen nodded dutifully. The queen looked frightened and the king noticed. "Dear, I think it would be important for you to set a good example in this," he told her. The queen nodded hesitantly.

"Good then. We're agreed. We will start this afternoon," the king said. "Now I'm going to have another serving of hashbrowns."

The queen's eyes widened. "Do you think that's a good idea?" she asked her husband.

The king was taken aback. "Well, I. I guess not," he stuttered.

The queen and her three children laughed until the king joined them.

Later that afternoon, the king went to find his family members to have them work out. He found the queen first in her study.

Chapter 29: Passive Voice

"Time to work out, dear!" the king said cheerfully.

The queen stifled a groan. "I was being inspired right as you came in."

"That's okay. You can come back to it after our workout," the king replied.

The queen sighed. "I will be worn out by then."

The king **disregarded** her argument and asked her to help round up the three kids to join them. They found Kirk lying on the sofa in the game room. He was watching a video on the screen.

★ ★ ★ ★ ★ ★ ★ ★ ★

disregarded – *ignored*
diminished – *reduced*

★ ★ ★ ★ ★ ★ ★ ★ ★

"Time for our workout! Let's go!" the king said enthusiastically.

"Already?" Kirk said. "I was being taught a lot about a new coding language."

"That's wonderful, Kirk. You can come back to it when we are done working out."

Kirk looked to his mother for help, but she just shrugged. The three of them left to find Luke and Ellen.

Ellen wasn't any more enthusiastic about working out than Kirk had been. "I was invited to a party by my friends," Ellen said in a whine. "The invitation is being sent to me right now."

"You can respond when we are finished with our workout," the king said firmly. He chose to ignore Ellen's pouting and took the family to get Luke.

Luke was lying on his bed, petting Comet. He wasn't happy to hear that it was time to work out, either. "I'm being entertained by Comet now. Can't we do it later?" he asked.

"Entertained? The dog isn't doing anything. We are working out now," the king replied.

The king's enthusiasm wasn't **diminished** by his family's reaction. He knew that once they got started working out, they would enjoy it.

In the castle's gym, the king demonstrated to everyone how to use the bench press. "At one time, people had to adjust the weights in this machine manually. Now the weight automatically increases or decreases to challenge but not exhaust you," he explained.

"Does it turn into a bed if you're too tired to lift weights?" Luke joked.

The king wasn't amused. "Luke, why don't you try it first? The machine will show us how much weight you're lifting."

"I'll be turned into a beast," Luke joked, flexing his chest. The rest of the family couldn't help but laugh. He lay down on the bench and begin to raise the bar easily at first. Then he was met with more resistance.

The king encouraged him to complete more reps. When Luke finished the set, he said, "I was wiped out by the bench press."

"It's good for you," the king said. "Your turn!" he said to his wife.

The queen was tempted to complain but knew it would do no good. She lay down on the bench and began pushing the bar. "This bar is being given a good workout by me," the queen said, gasping.

"Why did you say that?" the king asked, frowning.

"Why was a joke said by me?" the queen asked in an irritated tone. She got off the bench and gave her husband a look.

"Yes, that was funny," the king said with a phony laugh he hoped would appease his wife. "Kirk, your turn," he said, gesturing for his elder son to try the machine.

Kirk sighed. "I am being made late by this workout. How long will we be worked out by you?" he asked.

"Just do the set, Kirk," the king said, getting frustrated with the complaints. Kirk did a set of reps and the king complimented him on his strength. "Your turn, Ellen," he said, hoping that his daughter would comply without commenting.

But Ellen wasn't listening. She was messaging a friend on her communicator.

"Give me that," the king said tersely, taking the communicator from her. He read the message she'd written out loud. "'My day has been taken over by my father.' That's it!" the king roared. "You all know that exercise is important, right?" His family nodded apologetically. "Then why are you being so, so passive?" he asked with a sudden understanding.

He paced around the gym floor. "Dear, what did you say you did to this bar?" he asked the queen, grabbing the bar on the bench press.

"I am going to be criticized by you now?" she asked.

"No, just tell me what you said about it," he said more gently.

"It was being given a good workout by me," she repeated. "My jokes don't have to be appreciated by you," she said defensively.

"Dear, that's the passive voice," the king said.

"Now I'm being accused of being passive by you?" she said, her eyes filling with tears. "We are all being given high standards to meet here!"

"No, no, no. That's not what I mean. The matter will be cleared up by Screen. Ugh! Now I'm doing it! Let's go the library," he said, leading the way.

When the royal family was seated in the castle library, the king asked for a status report on planet Sentence.

Screen started a video of a sentence coordinator giving an interview. "The best way to ensure peace in the galaxy is to make our passive voices louder than the active ones," the coordinator said.

While she spoke, the camera panned people holding signs that read "Passive voices for peace."

The view switched to a reporter. "Sentence coordinators tell us that they are using passive voice whenever possible. The hope is that fewer conflicts will be the result."

The king was quiet when the video ended.

"Peace is a good thing, right?" Ellen asked tentatively.

The king tried to control the irritation he felt before responding. "Yes, peace is a good thing. But passive voice on planet Sentence has nothing to do with it. This is the Gremlin's idea and believe me, the last thing he wants is peace." The king removed *The Guide to Grammar Galaxy* from its place on the shelf, turned to the article on passive voice, and read it aloud.

Passive Voice

Passive voice is when the subject of a sentence is being acted upon. A sentence is in passive voice when a form of *be* (is, am, are, was, were, being, been) is paired with the past participle of the verb (i.e., the present or past perfect verb often ending in -ed).

The passive agent (that acts on the subject) may be added to the sentence with the word *by*.

Most telescopes **are manufactured** in China and Taiwan.

A new space program will **be launched** in two years.

Chapter 29: Passive Voice

> Pluto **was discovered by Clyde Tombaugh**. (passive agent)
>
> Verbs that cannot have direct objects are never in passive voice (e.g., arrive, come, die, go, live, sleep).
>
> **Active voice** emphasizes the subject as the acting agent.
>
> China and Taiwan **manufacture** the most telescopes.
> The country **will launch** a new space program in two years.
> Clyde Tombaugh **discovered** Pluto.
>
> **Use passive voice sparingly.** Active voice makes sentences easier to understand.

"I have been taught something new," Ellen said.

"That's passive voice, Ellen," the king said.

"I know! I hadn't been told about it before," she agreed.

The king sighed. "As you can see, passive voice has nothing to do with peace. Instead, we will be given more confusion and laziness. Ack! That was passive voice, too."

"We are being assigned a mission. Correct, Father?" Kirk asked.

The king nodded. "The sentence coordinators must receive instruction about passive and active voice. Most of our sentences should be written in active voice. Is that clear?" he asked.

"The workout will be skipped by us then?" Luke asked.

"For now, yes. But you will be reminded to work out when you return," the king said.

The children agreed and worked together on a mission for the guardians called Passive Voice.

What does *diminished* mean?

Which voice emphasizes the action of the subject?

Which voice was the queen using during her workout

Chapter 30

The queen was reading the latest issue of *Women's Universe* when she had an idea. The editor of the magazine had requested nominations of women who make the universe a better place. A few women would be chosen to receive an award and would attend a luncheon in their honor. The winners would also receive funds to be used in their charity work. She couldn't think of anyone more deserving of such an award than Cook.

Cook wasn't just in charge of the royal family's meals. She had also started a soup kitchen for the needy. She collected extra food from the castle, area restaurants, and grocery stores to supply the soup kitchen. As if that weren't enough, Cook also taught free classes in the community on how to make nutritious meals inexpensively.

There was just one problem. If she nominated her, the queen worried that Cook would be selected because of her royal **influence**. Cook wouldn't see it as a **legitimate** honor. The queen needed someone else to write an essay nominating Cook for the award. Fortunately, she knew just who to ask.

★ ★ ★ ★ ★ ★ ★ ★ ★ ★

influence – *authority*
legitimate – *real*
affirmation – *support*

★ ★ ★ ★ ★ ★ ★ ★ ★ ★

The queen found Ellen reading in her bedchamber. She sat down and showed her the magazine's request for nominations of women who make the universe a better place. When the queen explained that she wanted to nominate Cook, Ellen was delighted.

"That's a great idea!" she said, beaming. "She is so humble that she won't like the attention, but she deserves it."

"I'm so glad you feel that way, Ellen," the queen said, "because I was hoping you would submit the nomination."

"Me?" Ellen asked. "Why would I do it?"

She explained that Cook would assume she had been chosen for the award because the queen had nominated her. If Ellen nominated her, that was less likely. And even if she didn't receive the award, Cook would appreciate words of **affirmation** from Ellen even more than from the queen. "It would mean a lot to her, Ellen," the queen said.

"Hm. I know it would," Ellen said thinking. "I just have to send a letter to the magazine?"

"Not a letter exactly. It would be more like an essay. Will you do it?" the queen asked, eyes shining.

Ellen hesitated. She loved Cook and wanted to honor her. "Sure. I will," she agreed, smiling.

The queen high-fived her daughter.

"When do I need to send it?" Ellen asked.

"They don't list a deadline, but I think soon. We don't want to put it off and miss our chance to nominate her," the queen said.

"Right. I'll work on it," Ellen said energetically.

"One more thing. Let's keep it a secret, okay?" the queen said. "I want to surprise Cook, and I don't want her to say no to nominating her."

Ellen nodded. "Got it."

When her mother left, Ellen spent time thinking about all the reasons she loved Cook. She would write an amazing nomination that would be sure to win her the award. She put the magazine on her bookshelf to deal with later.

A few days later, the queen asked Ellen how her nomination was coming. "Ohhh, great! I have lots of ideas," Ellen said, realizing that she had forgotten all about it.

"Wonderful! Have you written them down?" the queen asked. Ellen hesitated. "I can see that you haven't. Get started today, okay?" Ellen nodded, embarrassed that she'd forgotten.

Ellen didn't have anything urgent to do, so she found her tablet and began making a list of all the things she loved about Cook. She had wrote:

1) She's nice.
2) She's funny.
3) She makes really good muffins.
4) She makes amazing cookies.
5) Her brownies are incredible.
6) Her cakes are so delicious.

Ellen read over her notes and frowned. She was getting hungry and she didn't feel good about how the notes were going. Would Cook win the award because she was good at baking? Should she list all the delicious foods Cook made?

She thought for a while longer and decided to go to the kitchen. She would be careful not to let on to Cook that she was doing research, but she needed more material.

When Ellen arrived in the kitchen, Cook was just removing a pan of warm snickerdoodle cookies. Ellen's mouth watered. Cook congratulated her on her excellent timing and encouraged her to pour herself a glass of milk while she waited for the cookies to cool.

It wasn't long before Ellen had sunk her teeth into a warm, buttery cookie. That gave her an idea. "Cook, what's the secret to a delicious snickerdoodle?" she asked.

"Hm. Good question. I would have to say cream of tartar. That's what gives it a tang that sets it apart from a sugar cookie. Why do you ask?"

Ellen stopped chewing and stared at Cook. She had to cover. "Uh, I was just thinking I could try making these for Kirk's birthday. I know he loves them as much as I do."

"That's a great idea! I'd be happy to give you the recipe," Cook said.

Whew! Ellen thought. *That was close.* She decided not to ask any more baking questions and give her intentions away.

Just then Ellen's communicator buzzed. She opened a message from Cher to see a picture of wall art she'd made for her room. Ellen showed the picture to Cook. "Isn't this cute? I want to make one, too!"

Cook agreed that it was cute and would look great in Ellen's bedchamber. Ellen left the kitchen to chat with her friend about wall art. Then she spent time searching for wall art images until she knew exactly what she wanted to create. But to get started, she had to get some supplies from the craft store.

She found her mother in her study. "We need to go to the craft store," Ellen gushed.

"To finish your nomination?" the queen asked.

"No, no, to make my wall art."

"What wall art?"

"I'm making wall art for my bedchamber like Cher made for hers. This is what I'm going to make," Ellen said, showing her an image on her communicator.

"I see. That's very nice," the queen said. "But it will have to wait until you finish your nomination."

"Can't I do the wall art first? It won't take me very long. I really want to go to the craft store," she pleaded.

"I'm afraid not. We want to be sure Cook is nominated in time to receive an award," the queen said firmly.

Ellen started to argue but thought better of it. "Okay. I'll go work on it now. But if I finish quickly, could we go to the craft store then?"

"I don't want you to rush this, Ellen. It's too important."

Ellen nodded and left the study. She walked toward her bedchamber, determined to finish the nomination quickly. But then she stopped. *I don't know how to write this essay*, she admitted to herself. She turned around and walked back to her mother's study and knocked on the door.

When the queen saw her, she warned Ellen not to ask about the craft store.

"No, this is about the nomination," Ellen said, sighing. "I don't know how to do it."

"To write an essay? You've written essays before," the queen said dismissively.

"I know. But what do I write? I love Cook, but I started making a list and I ended up with a bunch of great things she bakes! I'm going to mess this up," Ellen wailed, fighting off tears.

"Now, Ellen, don't get upset," the queen began.

"I *am* upset. I don't know what I'm doing!" Ellen answered, throwing her hands in the air in frustration.

"Ellen, it's not your fault."

"It's not?"

"No. I didn't teach you how to write a profile essay. You've written reports about people before, but this is different. I'm sorry I didn't prepare you. I guess I was so excited about nominating Cook that I didn't think about teaching you how to do it."

Ellen's shoulders sagged in relief. "You're going to help me?" she asked.

"Yes," the queen said, smiling. "But I want to teach your brothers as well."

The two of them found Kirk and Luke and went to the castle library with them. There the queen read them an article from *The Guide to Grammar Galaxy*.

Profile Essays

A profile essay is usually a written description of a person, but it may describe a place or event. While the essay is informative, it should also engage by telling a story from your perspective.

The first step in writing an excellent profile essay is to read published essays that are similar to what you plan to write. Note how the essay is organized as well as which parts grab your attention.

The second step in writing a profile essay of a person is interviewing your subject, if possible. In advance of the interview, you will want to create a list of open-ended questions (that cannot be answered with yes or no). You may ask about childhood, career, challenges, accomplishments, dreams, and more. The first questions should be simple to answer. As your subject becomes more comfortable, you can ask more personal questions. Be prepared to ask questions that aren't on your list. Take notes, but consider recording the interview so you can pay attention to what your subject is saying.

The third step in writing a profile essay is to decide how to present the material. Because the essay should tell a story, you may want to use a chronological structure. You could describe the person's childhood, career start, and current circumstances, for example. In most cases, you will want to organize your subject's story into three time periods. Alternatively, you can describe your subject under three topic areas. For example, you might describe a person's career, family life, and hobbies. Create an outline for your essay with notes about what you will describe under each section. Be sure to include direct quotes you want to use in the essay.

The fourth step is to write the essay. As with any essay, the introduction should grab the reader's attention. What is the most interesting or remarkable thing you can say about your subject? Describe it at the beginning of your essay. The body of the essay will be descriptive writing, sharing details that appeal to the five senses. Because the essay should also tell a story, make sure there is a problem your subject encounters that is solved or is in the process of being solved. The conclusion should summarize what you've described, clearly sharing your perspective on the subject of the essay. Referring back to what was shared in the introduction will make your essay feel complete.

The final step is to edit the essay. You will want to review your essay for spelling and grammar errors. But you will also want to have someone edit it for you. Ask

> your editor if there are parts that are dull or unclear. Make changes based on the feedback you get. If you are profiling a person, you may want to have your subject review your essay before submitting it for publication. That way any errors or objections can be handled before it's available to the public.

"Do I need to interview Cook?" Ellen asked when her mother was finished reading. "Won't that make her suspicious?"

"Not if you tell her you're learning to write profile essays," the queen said. Ellen seemed satisfied with her answer.

"I'm sure glad I don't have to write one of these essays. Sounds like a lot of work!" Luke joked.

"Thank you for reminding me," the queen said in a serious tone. "You'll be writing a profile essay, too."

"About Cook?" he asked in surprise.

"I would like to see you and Kirk write about other people who make a difference in the universe," the queen answered.

"I think we should have the guardians write profile essays, too. They wouldn't have to send them to *Women's Universe*, of course," Ellen said.

"I think that's a wonderful idea!" the queen said. "We can honor many people who are making a difference."

The three English children began creating a mission for the guardians called Profile Essays.

What does *legitimate* mean?

What is the first step in writing a profile essay?

Why didn't the queen blame Ellen entirely for putting off the essay?

Galactic Robotics Journal

Chapter 31

Kirk was elated when he read the letter from *The Galactic Robotics Journal*. He was being asked to serve as junior editor for the journal for a year.

The letter explained that he would read submissions to the children's section of the journal. He would give his opinion on their **caliber** and whether or not they should be published. Kirk knew he had been given an honor and he wanted to say yes. But he had to discuss it with his father.

★ ★ ★ ★ ★ ★ ★ ★ ★ ★ ★

caliber – *quality*

★ ★ ★ ★ ★ ★ ★ ★ ★ ★ ★

Kirk found the king out in the garden, watering some new flowers he'd planted. "Guess what?" Kirk said. "I've been invited to serve as junior editor for *The Galactic Robotics Journal*!"

"That's wonderful! I'm so proud of you, Kirk," the king said, hugging his elder son.

"Thanks," Kirk gushed. "I should say yes then?" he asked.

Chapter 31: Writing Summaries

"Hm," the king said, pausing. "Being an editor is a lot of work. It requires **substantial** reading. And that would be in addition to your studies and robotics competitions. If you commit to doing it, you can't quit if it gets to be too much. So think carefully before saying yes."

★ ★ ★ ★ ★ ★ ★ ★ ★

substantial – *a lot*
innovations – *inventions*

★ ★ ★ ★ ★ ★ ★ ★ ★

Kirk nodded. "I'll think about it," he said with less enthusiasm than he'd had.

"Whether you do it or not, it's a real honor to be asked," the king said to encourage him.

"Yes. And I would be the first to know about robotics **innovations**."

"That's true. I know it would be interesting work for you. And, of course, I like that it would help you grow as a reader and writer.

Kirk nodded again. "I'm going to tell Mother," he said, feeling positive once again.

The next day, Kirk told his father he had decided to accept the position.

"You're sure?" the king asked. "You'll be able to handle the extra reading in addition to your studies? You don't want to quit once you've started unless it's necessary."

"I know," Kirk said. "I can handle it," he said, standing a little taller.

"Okay. Tell them you accept. This is a big change for you," he said, smiling with pride.

Not long after Kirk accepted the position as junior editor of the robotics journal, he began receiving submissions. The king had been right. It was a lot of reading.

Kirk was eager to make a good impression on the senior editors, so he read new articles as soon as he received them. To understand the articles, Kirk used what he'd learned about nonfiction reading. He was first skimming the articles and looking at their subtitles and any images or charts included. Then he tried to make personal connections with the content. That helped him when he wasn't familiar with the topic.

But the journal wanted his recommendations on publishing the articles. That was the problem. He would start to write whether or not the journal should publish an article and he would stop. *What if he was wrong?* He was rereading the articles to be sure, but that didn't help.

He hoped that he could find articles that were easy to say yes or no to. So he would leave the articles he'd already read in a file, hoping that a decision would come to him later. Meanwhile, the journal kept sending him articles to read.

Kirk began to be stressed. He hadn't returned a single opinion on a journal article. He had other homework to do and robotics meetings several nights a week. His father had made it clear that he couldn't quit. And his father had warned him about the amount of work involved. How could he complain now?

The queen noticed signs of Kirk's stress. He refused family activities, saying he had work to do. He picked at his meals. And he seemed tired. She brought her concerns to the king.

"Have you checked with Kirk about how the journal editing is going?" she asked.

"Hm. Now that you mention it, I realize I haven't. I've had a lot going on lately. I'll talk to him about it," the king said reassuringly.

"I'm glad. Just remember that he may not want to admit he's struggling."

"That's a good reminder. You're a great mother," he said, kissing her on the cheek.

The king found Kirk in the computer lab. "Are you working on the journal articles?" he asked him.

"Yes," Kirk said, hunched over his keyboard.

"How many have they sent you?" the king asked.

"A substantial number," Kirk said, smiling ruefully.

The king couldn't help but chuckle. "I'm not here to say I told you so, Kirk. I'm here to help. Your mother is concerned about you."

Kirk's eyes watered and his throat ached as he tried to control his emotions. "I have been reading the articles as soon as I receive them."

"That's good! But?"

"But the journal wants my opinion on whether to publish them or not. I don't know if I'm right, and I don't even know how to write about them. So I put it off and by the time I'm ready to write I don't remember anything about the article," he said, putting his head in his hands.

"I see," the king said, putting his hand on Kirk's back to comfort him. "What you're doing isn't easy."

"It's not?"

"No. But I think I can help. If you write summaries of the articles, you'll not only have an easier time deciding whether they should be published, but you can also share the summaries with the senior editors so they can decide. The editors aren't leaving the decision entirely up to you, Kirk."

"They're not?" he asked with relief.

"No. But your summaries and opinions can save the senior editors a lot of time. Let's read what *The Guide to Grammar Galaxy* has to say about writing summaries."

Writing Summaries

A summary gives a clear, short description of the main points of an article, book, or lecture. Summaries are paraphrases (writing in your own words). Writing them is proven to help students understand and remember important information.

The introduction of a summary should include the author's name, title of the work, and the main idea presented.

A one-paragraph summary devotes separate sentences to each main point. Additional sentences may be used to explain the main points.

A multi-paragraph summary devotes at least a paragraph to each main point. Transition words (like *first, in addition,* and *finally*) are used to connect the paragraphs.

A concluding paragraph reviews the main points, connecting them to the thesis (main idea). If the summarizer gives an opinion of the work, it is shared here.

Annotating a written work may aid in writing a summary. Annotations involve highlighting the main points, circling new vocabulary words, noting reactions in the margins, and using symbols next to the text. Some common annotation symbols are listed below.

★	important
♥	favorite

Chapter 31: Writing Summaries

?	don't understand
!	surprising/interesting

"Do you think I could write a one-paragraph summary for each article?" Kirk asked.

"I think your editors would prefer that," the king said, smiling.

"I have a lot of work to do to summarize these papers," Kirk said, feeling overwhelmed.

"I bet you do. What if we had the guardians help you?" the king suggested.

"I can't give my work to them! The editors would think I was lazy," Kirk objected.

"Not if you explain that you want the guardians to know how to write summaries, too. What if you write one summary and then ask for permission to get the guardians' help?" the king said.

"What if they say no? Won't that make me look bad?" Kirk asked.

"I think they'll be impressed by the suggestion. But even if they're not, they will be happy to get your summaries."

Kirk thought it over and decided to write a summary right away. The king reviewed it and thought it was excellent. He told Kirk to send it to the editors and to suggest getting the guardians' help at the same time.

A senior editor responded the next day and loved Kirk's summary and his idea of getting the guardians involved. "We can use all the help we can get!" he wrote.

Kirk asked Luke and Ellen to help him create a mission called Writing Summaries.

What does *substantial* mean?

What is a summary?

Why did Kirk have a hard time making decisions about the journal articles he was reading?

Chapter 32

The royal family was on their way to an outdoor exhibit called Art in the Park. The weather was beautiful for it. Local artists and crafters of all sorts would be displaying their **wares**. The queen was looking forward to shopping, but she also thought it would be educational for the children.

★ ★ ★ ★ ★ ★ ★ ★ ★ ★

wares – *merchandise*
thronged – *crowded*
thwart – *prevent*

★ ★ ★ ★ ★ ★ ★ ★ ★ ★

The king had used their carriage as transportation. The queen had thought that would make the outing more fun. But now he was grumbling as the area around the park was **thronged** with people. "Dear, let's stay positive," the queen said, trying to **thwart** a fit of anger.

The king continued grumbling under his breath until he had found someone to care for his horses.

"Now we'll have a lovely time, won't we?" the queen said, taking her husband's arm.

"Yes," the king answered unconvincingly.

"Let's stop at each booth as we come to them," the queen suggested.

The king stifled a sigh.

The first booth the queen spotted had beeswax candles on display. The queen listened attentively as the woman explained the process they used to create the candles. First, they collected beeswax left over from honey collection. Then the beeswax was melted and impurities (dirt, pollen, etc.) were removed. The wax was poured into candle molds. Finally, a hot knife was used to smooth the finished candle in a process called burnishing.

"Aren't they beautiful?" the queen exclaimed.

"Yes, absolutely," the king said a little absent-mindedly.

Chapter 32: Persuasive Speaking

The queen ordered several of them but asked if she could pick them up on her way out of the park. While she waited to pay, she was dismayed to see the children using their communicators.

"We aren't here to use communicators, children," she chided them.

"I took a picture of the candles," Ellen said. "Look!" She showed her mother a photo of the candles she had taken with her communicator.

"Send that photo to me, will you?" the queen asked. "I want to show my friends how beautiful these candles are."

The family walked a short distance to another booth where the queen stopped to look. The booth displayed numerous hand-crafted bracelets. The queen was delighted with them. "Aren't they beautiful?" she exclaimed.

"Yes," the rest of the family murmured.

Ellen examined one of them closely and listened as a woman explained that the colorful beads were woven together by hand.

The queen decided to buy one for herself and let Ellen choose her favorite. While she was waiting for her choices to be packaged, she noticed that the boys were using their communicators. She elbowed the king to call his attention to that but noticed that he was also looking at his communicator.

"What are you doing?" the queen hissed.

"Oh, I'm checking my bank balance," the king joked.

"We are supposed to be spending time as a family and you're using communicators," the queen said so the boys could hear, too. The three of them put their communicators away while Ellen took a photo of her new bracelet with hers.

The queen had a hard time keeping her family's attention as she visited booths. It wasn't until she suggested getting lunch that everyone was engaged.

As the family enjoyed their food-truck meal, the king browsed the news on his communicator. "Hm. Parliament is considering banning communicator use for kids under 16," he said.

"What?" Kirk said indignantly. "I'm under 16. I need my communicator."

"Me, too!" Ellen said.

"Me three," Luke said, with his mouth full.

"They won't really take them away from us, will they, Father?" Ellen asked.

Chapter 32: Persuasive Speaking

"I don't know if they have the votes or not," the king replied.

"Judging by your behavior on this family outing, I have to say I think taking children's communicators away is a good idea," the queen said.

Kirk opened his mouth to respond and thought better of it.

After lunch, the rest of the family convinced the queen to cut their park visit short. It had become unbearably hot.

Once they had enjoyed a cool drink at home, Kirk asked to speak to the king privately. "I know Mother doesn't like us using our communicators so much. But I use my communicator for a lot of important things. I'm worried about Parliament taking them away from us," he said.

"I can understand that, Kirk," the king responded.

"Is there anything I can do to prevent them from going forward with this?" Kirk asked.

"Hm. It sounds like they are debating the issue in Parliament now. You could speak to them. As Guardian of the Galaxy, you would be allowed to speak."

"That would be great if you think it could make a difference," Kirk said, feeling a bit more positive.

"Oh, I do think it could make a difference. I'll make a few phone calls and arrange for you to speak."

"Thank you, Father," Kirk said, walking out of the room. "I'll wait to hear from you."

The king was proud of his son for being willing to defend his beliefs.

The next day the king told Kirk his opportunity to speak on the issue before Parliament had been arranged.

"That's great!" Kirk said, smiling. Then he frowned.

"What's wrong?" his father asked.

"What do I say?" Kirk asked, beginning to feel panicked.

"You say what you believe about kids and communicators," the king said in a tone that suggested the answer was obvious.

"Right," Kirk said, his left eye beginning to twitch. "Just say what I believe."

"Kirk, just give a persuasive speech," the king said matter-of-factly.

"Yes! Of course," Kirk said with a smile. Then he looked sober again. "I've never given a persuasive speech though, have I?"

"I haven't taught you how to give a persuasive speech?" the king said to himself. "What about? Wait, no. That wasn't really a persuasive speech. Well, Kirk, let's talk about how to give a persuasive speech then. But before we do, let's get your brother and sister involved. I have an idea."

After asking his younger children to join him in the castle library, the king read the article on persuasive speaking from *The Guide to Grammar Galaxy*.

Persuasive Speaking

A persuasive speech is one that seeks to change the audience's mind about a topic and potentially get them to take action. After researching your topic, there are three steps to writing an effective persuasive speech.

#1 Get the audience's attention. As with any speech, a persuasive speech's introduction should include attention-getters. Consider telling a story, sharing a surprising statistic, or using humor.

A bike helmet reduces the risk of cycling head injuries by more than 50%.

#2 Connect with the audience. The biggest obstacle to persuading may not be an opposing viewpoint but a lack of interest in the topic. A good persuasive speech helps the audience see why the issue matters to them. Speakers who create a personal connection with the audience through likability, relatability, or authority can also share why the issue matters to them.

Bike helmets aren't just for children. Approximately 88% of cyclists who die in crashes are adults. Most of the cyclists I treat in the emergency room weren't wearing helmets.

#3 Encourage action or a new attitude. First, present your audience's current viewpoint as though you agree with it.

Helmets may seem unnecessary if you're not riding in traffic.

Second, give information or examples that challenge your audience's viewpoint.

My son fractured his skull in a bike-trail accident. He wasn't wearing a helmet.

Finally, make the action you want your audience to take clear. Connect this call-to-action to the attention-getter in the introduction.

Wear a helmet every time you ride your bike, and you'll be far less likely to be one of the 80,000 people who will have a cycling-related head injury this year.

Practice until you feel comfortable enough to speak confidently without reading your speech. Record a video of yourself to check your posture and hand movements.

Chapter 32: Persuasive Speaking

"Kirk is going to give a persuasive speech to Parliament?" Luke asked.

"Yes, but that's not all," the king said. "I also want you two to speak to parents in your Grammar Girls and Guys groups."

"That's a great idea. But wouldn't we be even more persuasive if we had the guardians give speeches in their groups?" Ellen said.

"That's my girl!" the king said. "Brilliant idea."

"What if not all the guardians think kids should have communicators?" Luke asked.

"That's okay. The main thing is to get kids speaking and to have a discussion about it," the king said.

The children nodded and got to work on a mission called Persuasive Speaking.

What does *thwart* mean?

What is the second step in writing a persuasive speech?

Does the children's use of communicators at the park support taking them away? Why or why not?

Chapter 33

"Kirk, I have another request for your help," the king said. "I just received this letter from the editor of *The Grammar Gazette*. He would like you to write an article about the upcoming robotics competition. He knows that you'll be competing in it and he thought it would be good writing experience for you."

"Another honor," the queen said proudly.

"Yes. And I agree it will be good experience for you, Kirk. But do you have time for it?" the king asked.

"I am all caught up on journal editing and we are in good shape for the robotics competition. I shouldn't have a problem writing the article," Kirk said with a big smile.

"All right then. I'll have you contact the editor to work out the details," the king said.

"You're growing up too fast!" the queen **bemoaned**.

Kirk grinned and took the letter from his father. He went to the computer lab to email the editor that he accepted the assignment.

✯ ✯ ✯ ✯ ✯ ✯ ✯ ✯ ✯

bemoaned – *complained*
aura – *atmosphere*
meandered – *strolled*

✯ ✯ ✯ ✯ ✯ ✯ ✯ ✯ ✯

The next day the editor responded with delight that Kirk was willing to take the assignment. He said he wanted a report on the competition while it was ongoing. He explained that he hoped the article would entice more people to attend.

Kirk loved the idea. He loved having an audience for the competition. He thanked the editor and promised to send the article by the end of the first day's competition.

When Kirk walked into the arena where the robotics competition was being held, he could feel the **aura** of anticipation. Everyone was looking forward to the day's event.

Kirk's team's first match was early. One of his teammates arrived at the same time as Kirk, but the others hadn't yet arrived at the agreed-upon time. Kirk kept checking the time and began to feel stressed. *What if they didn't make it in time?* Kirk's anxiety became frustration as the rest of his teammates **meandered** into the arena.

"Where have you guys been?" Kirk asked, the veins in his neck bulging.

"What do you mean? We're here in plenty of time," one of them said. He looked to the other late arrivals as if to say he thought Kirk was overreacting.

"We have to get organized," Kirk said in a huff. "Do you have the battery charging station?"

"Uh, let me see," his teammate said, digging through the box he'd brought in. "Hm. I don't have it. Do you have it?" he asked another boy.

"No. I thought you had it," the boy responded.

"Great! That's just great!" Kirk said, pacing.

"Kirk, calm down. It's fine. We have plenty of batteries anyway," a teammate reassured him.

Chapter 33: News Articles

"Okay. I just want to make it to the finals," Kirk said, trying to get agreement from the other boys. But they were talking to one another and did not indicate that they were feeling the same way.

Kirk was agitated when his teammates neglected to turn the robot on before their first match. That resulted in a delay in the competition that made them look bad. That's how Kirk saw it anyway. He was relieved when they went on to win the match anyway.

In their next match, Kirk panicked when he couldn't find a spare part they needed. The pit was completely disorganized and his teammates didn't seem to care. When they eventually lost the match, Kirk lost his temper.

His coach had to step in. "Kirk, this is a practice match. Your teammates will not do better with you yelling at them," he said calmly. Kirk hung his head. "Remember that these are your friends and we are here to learn and have fun."

Kirk nodded that he understood. He apologized to his teammates and they told him he was forgiven.

When his team lost the next practice match, Kirk controlled his temper. But he was very upset. He had little to say when his family took him home that evening. Their reassurances weren't helping. He wanted to be in the finals and his teammates were impeding that.

Kirk went to his bedchamber early. He lay down and checked his email on his communicator, hoping some of his teammates had sent an apology for their attitude and lack of preparation. Instead, he found an email from the editor of *The Grammar Gazette* asking for his article on the robotics competition. He gasped and sat straight up in bed. *His article!*

Now he was really stressed. How could he possibly write a news article after everything that had happened? He would have to have his father make an excuse for him. He found the king reading in the media room.

Kirk was timid in bringing up the subject at first. "I just got an email from the *Gazette* editor, asking for my news article."

"Good grammar, I had forgotten about that," the king said, putting his book down.

"Yes, me too. Will you tell him I can't write it?" Kirk asked.

"I'll do no such thing!" the king exclaimed.

Chapter 33: News Articles

"What? I can't write a news article tonight! Especially after the day I've had," Kirk said wearily.

"Kirk, the newspaper is counting on your article. You can't ignore your commitment," the king said sternly.

Kirk sighed. "I don't even know *how* to write a newspaper article."

"You don't? I suppose this is the first time you've been asked to write one. I can help you with that part. But first, let's get Luke and Ellen to join us. I don't want to have to go through this with them a few years from now." The king smiled and put his arm around Kirk.

Later in the castle library, the king read the article on writing news articles from *The Guide to Grammar Galaxy* aloud.

News Articles

News articles answer the questions who, what, where, when, and how of current events.

To write a good news story, first read other stories as examples. Find news articles about similar events to review.

Next, be a part of the event, if possible. Attend the event and interview people who are involved in different ways. For example, you might interview a competitor, a fan, and an event organizer. Write down any quotes you'd like to use in the article, along with the names and roles of the people you interview.

The final step before writing the article is to outline it.
I. Begin with a hook to get the reader interested in the event.
II. Give basic facts about the event.
III. Share participants' perspectives on the event in the form of quotes and stories.
IV. Summarize and bring closure to the article. You may give another quote, invite readers to get involved, or share a source for more information.

As with any article, write a rough draft, read it aloud, and check it for spelling and grammar errors. News articles should be edited by others and the facts checked.

Kirk groaned. "I didn't interview anyone at the competition."

"You can message people and say you know it's short notice, but you'd love a quote from them about the competition," the king said.

"Yes, and I can give you a quote as an attendee," Ellen said.

"Okay, but what are you going to say?" Kirk asked nervously.

"I'll be nice," Ellen said, grinning.

Chapter 33: News Articles

"I'm going to have to apologize for my bad attitude again to get quotes from my team," Kirk said.

"I think that's a good idea anyway," the king said. "And even though it isn't typical to write about yourself in a news article, you can still write about how the competitors feel as an outside observer. Tell the reader the competitors' experience, which you learned today can be stressful."

"I can do that," Kirk said, smiling.

"Good luck getting your article done tonight," Luke said, smirking.

"Do you think you have the night free?" the king asked, smirking in return. "Think again. I want all the guardians to know how to write news articles. I'd like you and Ellen to put a mission together while Kirk works on his article."

"I was afraid you were going to say that," Luke said, sighing.

"It will be fun," Ellen said, elbowing him.

What does *bemoaned* mean?

What questions should a news article answer?

Why was Kirk stressed during the competition?

Chapter 34

"What?" the king exclaimed, losing his temper. He was reading the paper in the sunroom and his **outburst** disturbed the queen.

"Dear, lower your voice. You'll wake the children," the queen said.

"I can't this time. The platform of the candidate who is running in opposition to the prime minister is **intolerable**." The king had jumped up and was pacing the floor.

★ ★ ★ ★ ★ ★ ★ ★ ★ ★
outburst – *fit of temper*
intolerable – *unbearable*
★ ★ ★ ★ ★ ★ ★ ★ ★ ★

"I know the prime minister is your friend. But is the new candidate really that bad?" the queen asked innocently.

"That bad? Listen to this," the king growled, returning to the paper. "David Supplant, the frontrunner for the new Freedom Party, believes it is time for an English language with few, if any, rules."

"Fewer rules would be nice, though. Easier to teach, correct?" the queen said, hoping her husband would agree.

"That's not what they want. Don't you see?" the king said more angrily than he intended. "They want chaos in the galaxy. It's clear to me that Mr. Supplant is a Gremlin candidate. And freedom is not what we'll have if he's elected." He threw the paper down in disgust.

"Why don't you get a workout in?" the queen suggested hopefully. "You'll think more clearly."

The king was ready with an angry retort, but he stopped himself. "You're probably right." He left for the gym before he said something he would regret.

Later at breakfast, the king explained that a Gremlin candidate was opposing the prime minister in the election.

"Your father is very upset about it," the queen said, wanting her children to be supportive.

"The Gremlin never wins in this galaxy, Father," Luke said.

"That's right. People will see through him," Kirk agreed.

Chapter 34: Compare & Contrast Essays

"He does have better style than the Prime Minister," Ellen said, looking at the photo in the paper.

The queen gave Ellen a warning look.

"But the prime minister has a classic look that will never go out of style," she said to make up for her comment.

The king tried not to laugh but failed. Soon the rest of the family was laughing.

"I'm probably overreacting," the king admitted, feeling more at ease. "Cook!" he called out. "I'd love a second helping of waffles. I worked out hard." He smiled at his family around the table and told himself all would be well.

But the next evening at dinner, the king was again in distress. "They say Supplant is far ahead of the prime minister in the polls," he said.

"Polls aren't always accurate," Kirk replied.

"True. But what if they are this time?" the king said more as a statement than a question.

The queen saw a bead of sweat trickle down his forehead. She was more worried about her husband's mental state than about the upcoming election.

After dinner, she invited the children to the castle library, saying she wanted to read to them. The king was so **distraught** while watching the news that he didn't notice.

★ ★ ★ ★ ★ ★ ★ ★ ★ ★

distraught – *upset*

★ ★ ★ ★ ★ ★ ★ ★ ★ ★

"You see how upset your father is," the queen began. "I think there is a way you can help. I'd like you to write an essay comparing and contrasting Mr. Supplant and the prime minister as candidates."

"And you're going to tell us how to do that?" Kirk asked.

"Precisely," she answered, opening *The Guide to Grammar Galaxy*.

Compare & Contrast Essays
Compare-and-contrast essays discuss the similarities and differences between two subjects within the same category. For example, a compare-and-contrast essay of a book and movie only makes sense if they're the same title.

Chapter 34: Compare & Contrast Essays

Preparing to write your essay involves three steps.

1. Choose the two subjects for your essay. There should be enough similarities and differences between them to fill three to four paragraphs.

2. Research similarities and differences. Find examples of each to place in a Venn diagram (two overlapping circles in which similarities are written within the overlap).

3. Write an outline. In your introduction, explain why you are comparing the two subjects.

This comparison of these two mayoral candidates can help you confidently cast your vote on election day.

You may organize your points by topic, covering similarities and differences for each. For example, you may compare the setting of two books as one topic. Alternatively, you can present all the similarities and all the differences together. In your conclusion, give your thesis statement or opinion about the two subjects. Reflect on the attention-getter you used in the introduction, if possible.

While at first glance, the mayoral candidates seem quite similar, now you know you should cast your vote for Mr. X.

Next, write the first draft of your essay. Use your outline to guide you. Be sure to use transition words (e.g., next, in addition) between main points.

Finally, edit and proofread the paper. Check for spelling and grammar errors. Read your essay aloud. Have someone read your paper and tell you what your thesis statement was. If they aren't correct, revise your paper.

"How will we get people to read our essays on the prime minister candidates?" Ellen asked.

"I was thinking that you could publish them on your Grammar Galaxy Kids website," the queen said.

"But I don't think many parents read that site," Ellen said.

"Hm," the queen said, thinking. Then she smiled. "What if we ask the guardians to write compare-and-contrast essays, too?"

"Won't parents think we are trying to change their vote?" Kirk asked.

"Not necessarily. You won't require the guardians to write about this election. But you can certainly tell them you'll be sharing an essay about it on Grammar Galaxy Kids," the queen said.

"That could work," Kirk agreed.

"It could cheer your father up, knowing that you're doing what you can to help. And it has the added benefit of teaching the guardians how to write this type of essay," the queen said.

The English children sent out a mission called Compare & Contrast Essays. Then they got to work writing their own.

What does *distraught* mean?

Subjects of a compare-and-contrast essay must be in the same what?

Why is the king upset about the upcoming election?

Chapter 35

The king abruptly announced that he was taking Comet for a walk. The rest of the family looked at one another in surprise. He often suggested that one of the children take the dog for a walk. But they couldn't remember the king ever walking Comet by himself.

When he'd left, the queen told the children that he was still very upset about the election. David Supplant was leading in the polls by a wide margin over the **incumbent** prime minister.

★★★★★★★★★★
incumbent – *current*
★★★★★★★★★★

"I know he was hoping that your compare-and-contrast essay would help the voters see the truth. Instead, Mr. Supplant seems to be getting more positive media attention than ever. Your father is sure he is being funded by the Gremlin. And if he's elected, he will demolish everything we've worked for. Kids will stop reading, vocabulary words will weaken from lack of use, and bad grammar will be acceptable. Your father worries too much. But in this case, I understand his concern," the queen said.

"Is there anything we can do to help?" Ellen asked.

"You're so kind to ask, Ellen. I think we can all help by sharing the good things that are happening in the galaxy. Everything he reads and watches is negative now. He should know that bad news is what gets people's attention. That doesn't mean that the galaxy is falling apart," the queen said.

The children took what the queen had said to heart. When their father returned from his walk, they talked to him about the books they were reading. They knew it would cheer him up and it did.

At dinner that evening, the children reported on the guardians' progress. "I'm impressed with their writing," Kirk said. "I know you tell us that writing skills take years to develop, but the guardians have improved **immensely** this year."

"Yes, and I see them using new vocabulary words, too," Ellen agreed.

★ ★ ★ ★ ★ ★ ★ ★ ★ ★

immensely – *greatly*

derisive – *rude*

★ ★ ★ ★ ★ ★ ★ ★ ★ ★

"Even Cher? Or is everything still awesome and amazing?" Luke snickered.

"Luke, you're being **derisive**. How's that for a new vocabulary word?" Ellen retorted.

The queen suppressed a smile and told Luke to be kind.

"I see what you're doing," the king said in a serious tone.

"You do?" Luke asked.

"You're trying to cheer me up."

"And, did it work?" Luke asked.

"Yes," the king said with a big grin. "I am thankful for such a supportive family."

"We love you. And we think everything will work out," Ellen said, getting up to hug her father.

The king hugged his daughter back. "I'm sure you're right. Now, who would like to play tennis this evening?"

The family cheerfully agreed to play, thinking a little distraction would be good for all of them.

A few days later, the family took the tram to attend a professional spaceball game. It was family night at the stadium and the king loved that a meal was included in the ticket price. The queen loved it too because her husband wouldn't be complaining about how much he'd spent on food.

Other passengers on the tram stared at them, but the king didn't care. He said being with the fans was what made seeing the game in person better than watching on television.

They hadn't traveled far when Luke pointed out a billboard. It read "David Supplant for Prime Minister: Focused on Our Future."

The king was instantly incensed. He tried unsuccessfully to keep his volume low. "He shouldn't even be allowed to put up billboards!"

The queen took his arm and tried to calm him. "It's okay, dear."

"It isn't okay!" he hissed.

"I'm looking forward to the game!" Kirk said to divert his attention.

The king remained quiet as the rest of the family worried that he wouldn't enjoy the game.

When the tram stopped at the ballpark, the king led his family out and stopped to talk with them. "I'm sorry," he said, sighing. " I know better than to let politics ruin time with my family. Forgive me?"

"Of course we do!" the queen said as the children agreed. "Now let's go get our bargain meals," she said with a grin.

The king laughed and began talking with the boys about which pitchers would be starters.

It wasn't long before the king's mood had recovered completely. "I think this hot dog tastes better because it's cheaper," he joked. When he'd finished eating, he opened his program. His smile faded when he saw an ad for David Supplant. "Focused on our future," it read. His jaw clenched and he felt like ripping the program. But he looked at his wife and children and realized that he couldn't ruin their night. More specifically, he wouldn't let the Gremlin ruin it. He put the program away and enthusiastically participated in the wave as it went around the ballpark.

As the game progressed and the score was tied, the king forgot about Mr. Supplant. But between innings, the billboard ad they had seen while traveling appeared on the screen. "Look!" Luke said, pointing. When he remembered how upset it had made his father before, he put his hand down and grew quiet. He was surprised when the king said nothing.

In fact, the king said nothing about it for the rest of the game. He said nothing about it during the tram ride home. And he said nothing about it before he announced he was going to bed early.

The queen was the one who discussed it with the children that evening. "I want to do something to help the prime minister get reelected. I do believe the galaxy's future is more secure with him. And I know your father thinks so. Are you in?" she asked.

Her three children nodded and pledged their willingness to help.

"David Supplant has been successful in getting his name in front of the people. I've seen very few ads for the prime minister. But there's something else Mr. Supplant is doing that the prime minister isn't: He's using a slogan," the queen explained.

"What's a slogan?" Luke asked.

"I'm glad you asked," the queen said, smiling. She had the children follow her to the castle library. There she read the article on slogans in *The Guide to Grammar Galaxy*.

Slogans

A slogan is a short, memorable phrase used in advertising. Slogans are used to promote the advantages of a brand, cause, or political candidate over a competitor.

Slogans should be short. In general, use no more than eight words.
Just do it. – Nike

Slogans should be rhythmic. Use alliteration, rhyme, or song (jingle). People remember jingles the most.
The quilted quicker picker-upper – Bounty
I like Ike – Dwight D. Eisenhower's campaign slogan
"I'm a Big Kid Now" – jingle for Huggies

Use slogans to truthfully (without exaggeration) communicate:
An important benefit that sets the brand apart from the competition.
Nothing runs like a deer. – John Deere
The mission or goal.
We try harder. – Avis
Positive values and desires associated with the brand.
Win with Wilson – Woodrow Wilson's campaign slogan

Chapter 35: Slogans

> **Slogans are often associated with logos and taglines.** A logo is a symbol used to represent a brand. Taglines tend to be shorter and more descriptive. They are often printed with a logo.
>
>

"Are you saying that the prime minister needs a slogan?" Luke asked.

"Yes! Exactly," the queen answered.

"Doesn't he have a campaign reelection team for that?" Kirk asked.

"He should, but from what I can tell, they either haven't created one, or they haven't created a good one," the queen said.

"You'd like us to make a slogan for him," Kirk said.

"Yes, and I'd like you to help promote it any way you can."

"We can't ask the guardians to develop a slogan for the prime minister. But we can ask them to practice writing slogans. That will allow us to tell them what we're working on," Ellen said.

"Now you're thinking," the queen said, smiling.

What does *incumbent* mean?

How long should a slogan be?

What is one reason the queen believes the prime minister is behind in the polls?

Chapter 36

"It's Aunt Iseen's birthday next week, and I have a **glorious** idea," the queen said at breakfast. "Because her love language is meaningful words, I know she would love to have you children write something special for her."

glorious – *wonderful*
jab – *insult*
inspiration – *ideas*

"I can send her our compare-and-contrast essay," Luke joked. "Or the news article I wrote about the gaming competition I attended."

"Somehow I don't think that would be meaningful to her," the queen said, ruffling Luke's hair.

"You mean like a letter?" Ellen suggested.

"No. That would be nice, but I was thinking of a poem. I have a poem my father wrote for me when I got married that still means so much. Your aunt will treasure a poem," the queen said, getting misty-eyed.

"A poem? Like a haiku?" Luke asked.

"No, nothing like that, Luke," the queen said.

"But not an epic either, right Kirk?" Luke said, snickering.

"No, it doesn't have to be long," the queen said, ignoring Luke's **jab**.

"When do we need to have them done?" Kirk asked.

"I'd like to allow three days for them to arrive by mail. So that means I need them in three days. That will give me a day to help you edit them," the queen said. "I suggest you get to work right away."

Ellen and the two boys nodded but not enthusiastically.

Later that day, Luke went to the castle library to look through a book of poems for **inspiration**. He found one called "Love" by Victor James Daley. He read the first three stanzas.

Chapter 36: Gift Poems

> Love is the sunlight of the soul,
> That, shining on the silken-tress'd head
> Of her we love, around it seems to shed
> A golden angel-aureole.
>
> And all her ways seem sweeter ways
> Than those of other women in that light:
> She has no portion with the pallid night,
> But is a part of all fair days.
>
> Joy goes where she goes, and good dreams,
> Her smile is tender as an old romance
> Of Love that dies not, and her soft eye's glance
> Like sunshine set to music seems.

"Ugh. Maybe Aunt Iseen would like a poem like this, but I can't write one. I don't even know what it all means," Luke said aloud. He continued paging through the book but didn't see anything that would help him write a poem for his aunt. He decided to see what Ellen was going to do.

"It can't be that hard," Ellen said when he found her. "We've written poems before."

"Yes, but we can't write a haiku. Mother said so," he retorted. "What are you going to write in your poem?"

"I don't know, Luke. I haven't thought about it yet," Ellen said, getting annoyed with Luke's continued questions.

"Okay," Luke said, preparing to leave. "But tell me when you decide, okay?"

Ellen agreed that she would.

Luke had a similar conversation with Kirk. "What are you going to write?" Luke asked him.

"I don't know. I haven't decided," Kirk said impatiently.

"You know every time we put off writing we regret it."

"I know," Kirk said sighing. "But I just don't know what to write yet."

Luke thought about seeing if a few of his friends were up for a game of spaceball. Then he thought about how he would feel when his mother asked for his poem. She wouldn't be happy if he put it off, even though he'd sincerely tried to get an early start on it.

That's when he thought about what happened every time he didn't know what to do—about writing or any problem in the galaxy. He would eventually find the answer in *The Guide to Grammar Galaxy*. It was true that sometimes he needed his parents' help to know where to look. *But why shouldn't he try looking for help in the guidebook on his own?* he thought.

He returned to the library and looked up poetry in the book's index. He found a lot of articles they'd already read but one they hadn't called "Gift Poems." It sounded exactly like what he needed and it was.

Gift Poems

Poems make wonderful gifts. Consider writing one of these types of poems as a gift.

Acrostic poems. When given as gifts, these poems often use each letter in a person's name to begin a new line.

Odes. An ode is a short lyric poem used to praise someone or something. In ancient Greece, odes were set to music. The structure of odes varies, but they often rhyme.

English (Shakespearean) sonnets. Sonnets are 14-line poems made famous by Shakespeare. They use an alternating rhyme pattern in the first three 4-line stanzas. The final 2-line stanza is a rhyming couplet. English sonnets are often used to express romantic love.

Humorous. If your intended gift recipient has a good sense of humor, use rhyming lines that poke fun in a good-natured way. However, the poem should end with an expression of love for the recipient.

Once you've chosen the type of poem you'll write, begin making notes about your gift recipient. Include personality, work, hobbies, likes, dislikes, habits, memories with them, and positive aspects of appearance. (Note: Avoid poking fun at people's appearance.)

If you are writing a rhyming poem, use a rhyming dictionary to find words that rhyme with the words in your notes.

Write and revise your poem until it reads smoothly and with the right rhythm. Read it aloud and check for spelling and grammar errors. Always ask others who

Chapter 36: Gift Poems

> know the recipient to read the poem before you give it as a gift. You want to make sure that it will please the recipient. If you write the poem well, it will be a long-treasured gift.

"I'm so glad I don't have to write a sonnet for Aunt Iseen," Luke said to himself. He was sure she wouldn't want a romantic poem—not from him anyway.

He thought about how proud his mother would be when he was the first to turn in a poem. Kirk and Ellen would probably get into trouble for being late with theirs. He chuckled but then felt guilty.

Wouldn't his mother be even more proud of him if he taught his siblings how to write gift poems? That's what he'd do. And before anyone else could suggest it, he would say that they should write a mission on writing gift poems.

What does *inspiration* mean?

What is one type of poem that makes a good gift?

Why didn't Luke play spaceball?

About the Author

Dr. Melanie Wilson was a clinical psychologist working in a Christian practice, a college instructor, freelance writer, and public speaker before she felt called to stay home and educate her children. She is a mother of six and has homeschooled for more than 20 years. She says it's her most fulfilling vocation.

Melanie has always been passionate about language arts and used bits and pieces of different curriculum and approaches to teach her children and friends' children. In 2014, she believed she had another calling to write the curriculum she had always wanted as a homeschooling mom — one that didn't take a lot of time, made concepts simple and memorable, and was enough fun to keep her kids motivated.

Books have been a family business since the beginning. Melanie's husband Mark has been selling library books for over 30 years. Melanie and the older kids frequently pitch in to help at the annual librarians' conference. Grammar Galaxy is another family business that has been another great learning opportunity for their children.

When Melanie isn't busy homeschooling, visiting her kids in college, or writing, she loves to play tennis with family and friends.

Melanie is also the author of *The Organized Homeschool Life, A Year of Living Productively,* and *So You're Not Wonder Woman.* Learn more on her blog, Psychowith6.com, and her podcast, HomeschoolSanity.com.

About the Illustrator

Rebecca Mueller has had an interest in drawing from an early age. Rebecca quickly developed a unique style and illustrated her first books, a short series of bedtime stories with her mother, at age 9. Rebecca graduated with a BA in English from the University of Missouri - St. Louis with a minor in Studio Art in 2018 and is currently finishing her MLIS at the University of Missouri - Columbia.

Appendix: Answers to Comprehension Questions

Chapter 1
What does *wryly* mean? humorously

What are some subjects that students learn about when doing a literature unit study? language arts, history, geography, science, and art

Why were the other kings mad at the king of Grammar Galaxy? They thought he had sent them an arrogant, rude letter

Chapter 2
What does *infraction* mean? offense

How is mood created in literature? The setting, illustrations, and vocabulary are used to create mood.

Why did the English children have bad attitudes? On planet Composition, the mood of the month was set to bleak and sarcastic was the tone.

Chapter 3
What does *gratifying* mean? rewarding

Why were the books the English family read so short? Novels were turned into short stories because of the Short Story Statute

In short stories, less time is spent on developing what? the plot

Chapter 4
What does *ruminating* mean? pondering

What is an allusion? a figure of speech that indirectly refers to books, movies, people, or events.

Why did the member of Parliament want allusions removed from books? So no one is confused when hearing or reading them.

Chapter 5
What does *halfhearted* mean? unenthusiastic

What is a ballad? A short narrative poem often set to music

Why were the English children reading their poems with the wrong rhythm? The Gremlin had arranged for a new poetry conductor who emphasized the wrong beats

Chapter 6
What does *primes* mean? prepares

What is the first step in nonfiction reading comprehension? Read the title, subtitles, and glance at graphs/images and ask yourself what the reading is about.

Why did the king ban games and shows? He thought the kids' reading score would improve if they spent more time reading and less time on screens.

Chapter 7
What does *plausible* mean? believable

Why did Ellen want to leave the campground early? She was afraid of being bitten by a spider.

Why do you think urban legends are hard to disprove? People can say it happened to someone they know (friend of a friend)

Chapter 8
What does *merely* mean? only

What is the first step in understanding a Shakespearean play? Read a plot synopsis.

Why was Luke struggling to enjoy *Hamlet*? He hadn't used any of the steps to understanding it before reading.

Chapter 9
What does *flabbergasted* mean? stunned

What is a parody? Satire in the form of imitation

Why did the English children believe the article about their father was true? It was on a news site and they didn't think it would publish libel.

Chapter 10
What does *sputtering* mean? stammering

What is one way to learn new science vocabulary words? Regularly reading science materials; adding new words to a notebook; playing vocabulary games; using the words in conversation

Why didn't Ellen want to participate in the science fair? She didn't understand science vocabulary or think she was good at science.

Chapter 11
What does *incongruity* mean? oddness

What is an oxymoron? Oxymorons are figures of speech that are a combination of literal opposites.

Why do you think the king wanted to work out longer than usual? He had been teased with the words "jumbo" and "larger."

Chapter 12
What does *soothe* mean? soothe

What is one type of onomatopoeia sound? Collision, animal, vocal, water, air

Why didn't the students hear the tram accident? Because of the Onomatopoeia Union strike

Chapter 13
What does *shamefaced* mean? embarrassed

What is one spelling difference between British and American English? -our/-or Unstressed ending syllables are spelled -our in British English and -or in American English. **-re/-er** British words ending in -bre or -tre are spelled -ber or -ter in American English. **-ise/-ize** British English mostly uses -ise at the end of words while American English uses -ize. **-ll/-l** British and American English use a double ll for different words. **-e** British English often keeps a silent -e when adding a suffix, whereas American English does not.

Why did Happy Holographics correct Luke's spelling? They wanted British spelling.

Chapter 14
What does *requisite* mean? necessary

What is the barrister's job? attorney

Why are there differences in American and British vocabulary? Language changes develop as people live separately.

Chapter 15
What does *impertinent* mean? disrespectful

What word should Luke have used instead of *supposably*? supposedly

What event was happening on planet Vocabulary that caused wrong words to be used? Masquerade ball

Chapter 16
What is a quandary? dilemma

What is one way to remember the meaning of a vocabulary word? sayings, word pictures, songs, premade mnemonics

Why did Luke assume Cook was calling him a dummy? He felt dumb that he couldn't remember his vocabulary words.

Chapter 17
What does *profusely* mean? abundantly

Why was the king unable to finish some words? The suffixes he needed were working at the theme park and weren't available for use.

What suffix is missing in the king's question, 'Does that make you nerv—'? -ous

Chapter 18
What does *shrill* mean? high-pitched

What is the Fry Word List? The Fry Word List, compiled by Dr. Edwin Fry, includes the 1,000 most-used words in reading material from grades 3-9.

Why didn't Luke want to text message his friends? He was afraid of making a spelling mistake and being teased.

Chapter 19
What is a concession? A deal

What must you know first to diagram a sentence? Parts of speech

Why was the king upset about the newspaper article? He thought people would be happy he was teaching diagramming, and they weren't.

Chapter 20
What does *amenable* mean? agreeable

How many main types of grammatical mood are there? five

What was the grammatical mood of the day when the queen was directing the family to do chores? Imperative

Chapter 21
What does *endeavor* mean? effort

How can you fix a split infinitive? Place the adverb before or after the infinitive.

Why doesn't the king like the phrase 'to boldly go'? It's a split infinitive.

Chapter 22
What does *usurp* mean? take

What is unique about the progressive tense? It's used to show that a verb's action is in progress and ongoing.

How do you think the king will react when he learns the children have sent out a progressive tense mission? He will be unhappy at best and angry at worst.

Chapter 23
What does *intoned* mean? spoke

What is the difference between an adverbial clause and phrase? Clauses include both a subject and predicate and phrases do not.

How do you think the words on planet Sentence will respond when the king stops *TheyDunnit* from airing there? They will be upset.

Chapter 24
What does *vexation* mean? annoyance

What are some examples of relative pronouns? that, which, who, whose, whom

Why was the queen stuttering at the reunion? She couldn't use relative pronouns that continue her thoughts.

Chapter 25
What does *favorable* mean? positive

Why is "hot guardians' mess" a misplaced modifier? Instead of the mess being hot or significant, the guardians are described as hot.

Was the *Galaxy Life* article likely to improve the king's approval rating? No. It made him sound like a lazy.

Chapter 26
What does *steeled* mean? strengthened

What is the difference between an en and em dash? The en dash is shorter and is used to show a range. The em dash is used to replace, colons, parentheses, and missing information.

Will using more dashes and parentheses prevent run-on sentences? No.

Chapter 27
What does *subdued* mean? quiet

Why does parallelism matter? It makes sentences easier to read and understand.

Why is this sentence not parallel? *He takes any opportunity to lie, confuse, and to cause problems.* To be parallel, confuse should be the infinitive to confuse.

Chapter 28
What is a *pastime*? A hobby

Why didn't Cook want the queen to edit Luke's morning pages? Because it could keep him from being motivated to write.

How many pages should you write when completing morning pages? three

Chapter 29
What does *diminished* mean? reduced

Which voice emphasizes the action of the subject? active

Which voice was the queen using during her workout? passive

Chapter 30
What does *legitimate* mean? real

What is the first step in writing a profile essay? Reading published essays that are similar to what you plan to write.

Why didn't the queen blame Ellen entirely for putting off the essay? She hadn't taught her how to write a profile essay.

Chapter 31
What does *substantial* mean? a lot

What is a summary? A clear, short description of the main points of an article, book, or lecture.

Why did Kirk have a hard time making decisions about the journal articles he was reading? He thought the decision was up to him and he didn't know about writing summaries to help.

Chapter 32
What does *thwart* mean? prevent

What is the second step in writing a persuasive speech? Connect with the audience.

Does the children's use of communicators at the park support taking them away? Why or why not? Answers will vary.

Chapter 33
What does *bemoaned* mean? complained

What questions should a news article answer? who, what, where, when, and how of current events

Why was Kirk stressed during the competition? He wanted to make it to the finals, especially because he was writing a news article about the competition.

Chapter 34
What does *distraught* mean? upset

Subjects of a compare-and-contrast essay must be in the same what? category

Why is the king upset about the upcoming election? His friend, the prime minister, is behind a Gremlin candidate in the polls.

Chapter 35
What does *incumbent* mean? current

How long should a slogan be? No more than eight words.

What is one reason the queen believes the prime minister is behind in the polls? Few ads and no slogan.

Chapter 36
What does *inspiration* mean? ideas

What is one type of poem that makes a good gift? Acrostic, ode, sonnet, humorous

Why didn't Luke play spaceball? He knew his mother wouldn't be happy if he put off writing the poem

Made in the USA
Monee, IL
03 April 2024

55689270R00109